LORENA WEISS

W9-DDP-533

VISUAL QUICKSTART GUIDE

JAVASCRIPT

FOR THE WORLD WIDE WEB

2ND EDITION

Tom Negrino
Dori Smith

 Peachpit Press

Visual QuickStart Guide
JavaScript for the World Wide Web, 2nd Edition
Tom Negrino and Dori Smith

Web site for this book: http://www.chalcedony.com/javascript/

Peachpit Press

1249 Eighth Street
Berkeley, CA 94710
(800) 283-9444
(510) 524-2178
(510) 524-2221 (fax)

Find us on the World Wide Web at: http://www.peachpit.com

Peachpit Press is a division of Addison Wesley Longman

Copyright © 1998 by Tom Negrino and Dori Smith

Editor: Nancy Davis
Production: David Van Ness
Inhouse production: Amy Changar
Cover design: The Visual Group

Notice of rights
All rights reserved. No part of this book may be reproduced or transmitted in any form or by any means, electronic, mechanical, photocopying, recording, or otherwise, without prior written permission of the publisher. For more information on getting permission for reprints and excerpts, contact Trish Booth at Peachpit Press.

Notice of liability
The information in this book is distributed on an "As is" basis, without warranty. While every precaution has been taken in the preparation of this book, neither the author nor Peachpit Press shall have any liability to any person or entity with respect to any loss or damage caused or alleged to be caused directly or indirectly by the instructions contained in this book or by the computer software and hardware products described herein.

ISBN: 0-201-69648-7

0 9 8 7 6 5 4 3

Printed and bound in the United States of America

Dedication

To the memory of
Bill Horwitz and Dorothy Negrino,
because they loved learning.

Thanks!

Our heartfelt thanks to our editor Nancy Davis, for a wonderful experience (our first with Peachpit; we'll be back). Thanks also to Nolan Hester, who got us started, and to the rest of the Peachpit staff who helped out.

To our agent, Brian Gill of Studio B, thanks for the hard work and good advice.

To our son Sean, for understanding when his parents got cranky, and for not grumbling too much about those missed bedtime stories.

Tom would like to thank (once again) Linda Comer and Anita Epler at *Macworld* magazine.

Dori would like to thank Lexy Scott, Doug Dawirs, and Drea Solan at The Workbook for their support and understanding, and the wonderful ladies in the W&S group for their loving kindness and virtual hugs.

Thanks also to the team at Connectix that produced the terrific Virtual PC, saving us from having to go out and buy a new computer.

TABLE OF CONTENTS

INTRODUCTION

Welcome to JavaScript! Using this easy-to-learn programming language, you'll be able to add pizzazz to your Web pages and make them more useful for you and for your site's visitors. We've written this book as a painless introduction to JavaScript, so you don't have to be a geek or a nerd to write a script. Pocket protectors will not be necessary at any time. As a friend of ours says, "We're geeky, so you don't have to be!"

We wrote this book for you

We figure that if you're interested in JavaScript, then you've already got some experience in creating HTML pages and Web sites, and you want to take the next step and add some interactivity to your sites. We don't assume that you know anything about programming or scripting. We also don't assume that you are an HTML expert (though if you are, that's just fine). We do assume that you've got at least the basics of building Web pages down, and that you have some familiarity with common HTML like links, images, forms, and frames.

How to use this book

Throughout the book, we've used some devices that should make it easier for you to work with both the book and with JavaScript itself.

In the step-by-step instructions that make up most of the book, we've used a special type style to denote either HTML or JavaScript code, like this:

```
<BODY>
window.status
```

You'll also notice that we show the HTML in uppercase, and the JavaScript in lowercase, which makes it easier to distinguish between the two on a Web page. Whenever you see a quote mark in a JavaScript, it is always a straight quote (like ' or "), never curly quotes (aka "smart" quotes, like ' or ").

In the illustrations accompanying the step-by-step instructions, we've highlighted the part of the scripts that we're discussing in red, so you can quickly find what we're talking about. We often also highlight parts of the screen shots of Web browser windows in red, to indicate the most important part of the picture.

Because book pages are narrower than computer screens, some of the lines of JavaScript code are too long to fit on the page. When this happens, we've broken the line of code up into one or more segments, inserted this gray arrow → to indicate that it's a continued line, and indented the rest of the line. Here's an example of how we show really long lines in scripts.

```
document.write("You're running Netscape
 → Navigator, a fine JavaScript-enabled browser.")
```

Don't type that code!

Some books give you program listings, and expect you to type in the examples. We think that's way too retro for this day and age. It was tough enough for us to do all that typing, and there's no reason you should have to repeat that work. So we've prepared a companion Web site for this book, one that includes all of the scripts in the book, ready for you to just copy and paste into your own Web pages. The site also includes additional tips and scripts. If we discover any mistakes in the book that got through the editing process, we'll list the updates on the site, too. You can find our companion site at:

http://www.chalcedony.com/javascript/

If for some reason you do plan to type in some script examples, you might find that the examples don't seem to work, because you don't have the supporting files that we used to create the examples. For example, in an example where a sound plays when you click an on-screen button, you'll need a sound file. No problem. We've put all of those files up on the book's Web site, nicely packaged for you to download. You'll find one downloadable file per chapter, containing all of the scripts, HTML files, and the sound and image files we used in that chapter.

You can contact us via e-mail at:
javascript-vqs@chalcedony.com

Time to get started

One of the best things about JavaScript is that it's easy to start with a simple script that makes cool things happen on your Web page, then add more complicated stuff as you need it. You don't have to learn a whole book's worth of information before you can start improving your Web pages.

Of course, every journey begins with the first step, and if you've read this far, your journey into JavaScript has already begun. Thanks for joining us, and please keep your hands and feet inside the moving vehicle. And please, no flash photography.

GETTING ACQUAINTED WITH JAVASCRIPT

For Web site creators, the evolution of HTML has been a mixed blessing. In the early days of the World Wide Web, HTML was fairly simple, and it was easy to learn most everything you needed to learn about putting together Web pages.

As the Web grew, page designers' aspirations grew as well, and their demand for greater control over the look of the page forced HTML to change and become more complex.

Because the Web is a dynamic medium, page designers also wanted their pages to interact with the user, and it soon became obvious that HTML was insufficient to handle the demand. Netscape invented JavaScript as a way to control the browser and add flash and interactivity to Web pages.

In this chapter, you'll learn what JavaScript is (and what it isn't); what it can do (and what it can't); and some of the basics of the JavaScript language.

What JavaScript is

JavaScript is a programming language that you can use to add interactivity to your Web pages. But if you're not a programmer, don't panic at the term "programming language"; there are lots of JavaScripts available on the Web that you can copy and modify for your own use with a minimum of effort. In fact, standing on the shoulders of other programmers in this way is a great technique for getting comfortable with JavaScript, and if you do enough of it (and read this book), you'll soon be creating your own scripts from scratch.

To make it easier for you to get up and running with JavaScript, the authors have set up a Web site that supplements this book. We've included all the scripts in the book (so you don't have to type them in yourself!), as well as additional notes, addendums, and updates. You can find our site at http://www.chalcedony.com/javascript/.

You'll often see JavaScript referred to as a "scripting language," with the implication that it is somehow easier to script than to program. It's a distinction without a difference, in this case.

A JavaScript script is a program that is included on an HTML page. Because it is enclosed in the <SCRIPT> tag, the text of the script doesn't appear on the user's screen, and the Web browser knows to run the JavaScript program. The <SCRIPT> tag is most often found within the <HEAD> section of the HTML page, though you can, if you wish, have scripts in the <BODY> section. Scripts that write text to the screen or that write HTML are best put in the <BODY> section, as in Script 1.1. If you're unfamiliar with these HTML concepts and you need more information about HTML, we suggest that you check out Elizabeth Castro's *HTML for the World Wide Web: Visual Quickstart Guide*, also available from Peachpit Press.

Script 1.1 This very simple script types "Hello, Cleveland!" into the browser window.

```
<HTML>
<HEAD>
<TITLE>Barely a script at all</TITLE>
</HEAD>
<BODY BGCOLOR=WHITE>
<H1>
<SCRIPT>
    document.write("Hello, Cleveland!")
</SCRIPT>
</H1>
</BODY>
</HTML>
```

Figure 1.1 A rollover is an image that changes when you move the mouse pointer over it.

What JavaScript can do

There are many things that you can do with JavaScript to make your Web pages more interactive and provide your site's users with a better, more exciting experience.

JavaScript lets you create an active user interface, giving the users feedback as they navigate your pages. For example, you've probably seen sites that have buttons that highlight as you move the mouse pointer over them. That's done with JavaScript, using a technique called a *rollover* (Figure 1.1).

You can use JavaScript to make sure that your users enter valid information in forms, which can save time and money. If your forms require calculations, you can do them in JavaScript on the user's machine without needing to use a complex server CGI (a program that runs on a Web server and extends the server's functions).

With JavaScript, you have the ability to create custom HTML pages on the fly, depending on actions that the user takes. Let's say that you are running a travel site, and the user clicks on Hawaii as a destination. You can have the latest Hawaii travel deals appear in a new window.

JavaScript controls the browser, so you can open up new windows, display alert boxes, and put custom messages in the status bar of the browser window.

Because JavaScript has a set of date and time features, you can generate clocks, calendars, and timestamp documents.

In Netscape Navigator 3.0 and Microsoft Internet Explorer 3.0 and later, you can use JavaScript to test for the presence of browser plug-ins, and direct the user to a different page if they don't have the plug-in needed to view your page.

JavaScript isn't Java

Despite the name, JavaScript and Java have almost nothing to do with one another. Java is a full-featured programming language developed and marketed by Sun Microsystems. With Java, a descendant of the C and C++ programming languages, programmers can create entire applications and control consumer electronic devices, much as C and C++ are used. Unlike those languages, Java holds out the promise of cross-platform compatibility, that is, a programmer should be able to write one Java program that could then run on any kind of machine, whether that machine is running Windows 95 or NT, the Mac OS, or Unix. In practice, Java hasn't fully realized that dream, due in no small part to bickering between Sun and Microsoft as to the direction of the language. Microsoft got involved because they want to integrate Java into Windows in their own way (a way that Sun says would make Java work one way on Windows, and another way on other machines, thereby defeating Java's main purpose).

Java's main use is to create *applets*, small programs that download over the Internet and run inside Web browsers. Because of Java's cross-platform nature, these applets should run identically on any Java-enabled browser (a browser that has the Java engine built-in).

You embed Java applets in your Web pages using the **APPLET** HTML tag. When the browser sees the **APPLET** tag, it downloads the Java applet from the server, and the applet then runs in the area of the screen specified in the tag (Figure 1.2). When the user moves on to another Web page, the applet is flushed from the computer's memory.

JavaScript can interact with a Java applet on a Web page, as you'll see in Chapter 9. The combination of JavaScript and Java enables you to provide a powerful and interesting experience to your site's users.

Figure 1.2 This Java applet plays a mean game of checkers, and is something you can't create with JavaScript. The applet takes up the space from the pop-up menus for player color, down to the buttons at the bottom of the screen.

4

Figure 1.3 The cat object (this one's name is Pixel).

Figure 1.4 This pop-up menu is a browser object, which can be manipulated by JavaScript.

The snap-together language

Here's another buzzword that we should get out of the way: JavaScript is an *object-oriented* language. So what does that mean?

Objects

First, let's think about objects. An *object* is some kind of a thing. A cat, a computer, and a bicycle are all objects (Figure 1.3) in the physical world. To JavaScript, there are objects it deals with in Web browsers, such as windows, forms, and the elements of the form, such as buttons and check boxes (Figure 1.4).

Because you can have more than one cat, or more than one window, it makes sense to give them names. While you could refer to your pets as Cat #1 and Cat #2, it's a bad idea for two reasons: first, it's easier to tell the cats apart if they have unique names, and second, it's just plain impolite. In the same way, all the examples in this book will give objects their own unique names.

✔ Tip

- Be aware that scripts you might see on the Internet will refer to objects like window[0] and form[1]. This is poor style for the reasons given above, and you'll find that it's much easier for you to keep track of the different objects in your scripts if you give them names instead of numbers.

Properties

Objects have *properties*. A cat has fur, the computer has a keyboard, and the bicycle has wheels. In the JavaScript world, a window has a title, and a form has a check box.

Properties can modify objects, and the same property can apply to completely different objects. Let's say that you have a property called empty. It's okay to use empty wherever it applies, so you could say that both the cat's tummy is empty and the cat's bowl is empty.

Note that the computer's keyboard and the bicycle's wheels aren't only properties; they are also objects in their own right, which can have their own properties. So objects can have sub-objects.

Methods

The things that objects can do are called *methods*. Cats purr, computers crash, and bicycles roll. JavaScript objects also have methods: buttons click( ), windows open( ), and text can be selected( ). The parentheses signal that we're referring to a method, rather than a property.

✔ Tip

- It might help to think of objects and properties as nouns, and methods as verbs. The former are things, and the latter are actions that those things can do, or have done to them.

Putting the pieces together

You can put together objects, properties, and methods to get a better description of an object, or to describe a process. In JavaScript, these are separated by periods (also known as dots, as in Internet addresses). This is called *dot syntax*. Here's some examples of objects and their properties written in this way:

```
bicycle.wheels
cat.paws.front.left
computer.disk.floppy
document.images.name
window.status
```

And here are some examples of objects and methods written in dot syntax:

```
cat.purr()
document.write()
forms.elements.radio.click()
```

THE SNAP-TOGETHER LANGUAGE

Handling Events

Events are actions that the user performs while visiting your page. Submitting a form and moving a mouse over an image are two examples of events.

JavaScript deals with events with commands called *event handlers*. An action by the user on the page triggers an event handler in your script. The twelve JavaScript event handlers are listed in Table 1.1.

For example, let's say that our cat handles the event onPetting( ) by performing the actions purr and stretch.

In JavaScript, if the user clicks on a button, the onClick( ) event handler will take note of the action and perform whatever duties it was assigned.

When you write a script, you don't have to anticipate every possible action that the user might take, just the ones where you want something special to occur. For instance, your page will load just fine without an onLoad( ) event handler. But you would use the onLoad( ) command if you want to trigger a script as soon as the page loads.

Table 1.1

Event Handlers	
EVENT	**WHAT IT HANDLES**
onAbort	The user aborted loading the page
onBlur	The user left the object
onChange	The user changed the object
onClick	The user clicked on an object
onError	The script encountered an error
onFocus	The user made an object active
onLoad	The object finished loading
onMouseOver	The cursor moved over an object
onMouseOut	The cursor moved off an object
onSelect	The user selected the contents of an object
onSubmit	The user submitted a form
onUnload	The user left the window

Table 1.2

Value Types		
TYPE	**DESCRIPTION**	**EXAMPLE**
Number	Any numeric value	3.141592654
String	Characters inside quote marks	"Hello, world!"
Boolean	True or False	True
Null	Empty and meaningless	
Object	Any value associated with the object	
Function	Value returned by a function	

Table 1.3

Operators	
OPERATOR	**WHAT IT DOES**
x + y (Numeric)	Adds x and y together
x + y (String)	Concatenates text x and text y together (i.e., concatenating "check" and "box" produces "checkbox")
x – y	Subtracts y from x
x * y	Multiplies x and y together
x / y	Divides x by y
x % y	Modulus of x and y (i.e., the remainder when x is divided by y)
x++, ++ x	Adds one to x (same as x = x + 1)
x– – , – – x	Subtracts one from x (same as x = x – 1)
–x	Reverses the sign on x

Values and variables

In JavaScript, a piece of information is a *value*. There are different kinds of values; the kind you're most familiar with are numbers. A *string* value is a word or words enclosed in quotes. Other kinds of JavaScript values are listed in Table 1.2.

Variables contain values. For example, the variable myName is assigned the string "Dori." Another way to write this is myName = "Dori". The equals sign can be read as "is set to." In other words, the variable myName now contains the value "Dori."

✔ Tips

- JavaScript is case sensitive. This means that myname is not the same as myName, and neither is the same as MyName.

- Variable names cannot contain spaces or other punctuation. They also can't be one of the JavaScript reserved words. See Appendix B for a list of JavaScript reserved words.

Operators

Operators are the symbols used to work with variables. You're already familiar with operators from simple arithmetic; plus and minus are operators. See Table 1.3 for the full list of operators.

✔ Tips

- While both x++ and ++x add one to x, they are not identical; the former increments x after the assignment is complete and the latter before. For example, if x is 5, "y = x++" results in y set to 5 and x set to 6, while "y = ++x" results in both x and y set to 6. The operator "––" works similarly.

- If you mix numeric and string values when adding two values together, the result is a string. For example, "cat" + 5 results in "cat5".

Assignments and comparisons

When you put a value into a variable, you are assigning that value to the variable, and you use an assignment operator to do the job. For example, you use the equals operator to do an assignment, such as hisName = "Tom". There are a whole set of assignment operators as listed in Table 1.4.

Other than the equals sign, the other assignment operators serve as shortcuts for modifying the value of variables. For example, a shorter way to say "x=x+5" is to say "x+=5". For the most part, we've used the longer version in this book for clarity's sake.

Comparisons

You'll often want to compare the value of one variable with another, or the value of a variable against a literal value (i.e., a value typed into the expression). For example, you might want to compare the value of the day of the week to "Tuesday," and you can do this by checking if todaysDate == "Tuesday". A complete list of comparisons is in Table 1.5.

✔ Tip

■ If you are comparing strings, be aware that "a" is greater than "A" and that "abracadabra" is less than "be".

Table 1.4

Assignments

ASSIGNMENT	WHAT IT DOES
x = y	Sets x to the value of y
x += y	Same as x = x + y
x – = y	Same as x = x – y
x * = y	Same as x = x * y
x / = y	Same as x = x / y
x % = y	Same as x = x % y

Table 1.5

Comparisons

COMPARISON	WHAT IT DOES
x == y	Returns true if x and y are equal
x != y	Returns true if x and y are not equal
x > y	Returns true if x is greater than y
x >= y	Returns true if x is greater than or equal to y
x < y	Returns true if x is less than y
x <= y	Returns true if x is less than or equal to y
x && y	Returns true if both x and y are true
x || y	Returns true if either x or y is true
!x	Returns true if x is false

ASSIGNMENTS AND COMPARISONS

Figure 1.5 WordPad on Windows 95.

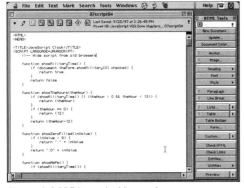

Figure 1.6 BBEdit on the Macintosh.

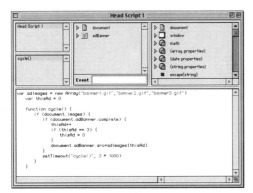

Figure 1.7 CyberStudio on the Macintosh.

What tools to use?

Since JavaScript is just plain text, you could use almost any kind of text editor. You could even use a word processor like Microsoft Word, though you would always have to make sure that Word saved the file as Text Only, instead of in its native file format, which can't be read by a Web browser (not even Microsoft's Internet Explorer).

You're better off using a program that has plain text as its standard format. On Windows 95, many people use WordPad (Figure 1.5). On the Mac, you could use SimpleText, though a favorite of professionals is BBEdit, by Bare Bones Software (Figure 1.6). On Unix machines, Emacs is one of the best text editors available. No matter what program you use, don't forget to save your plain text files with the extension .html or .htm so that things will go smoothly when you upload the file to a Web server.

You can also use some of the WYSIWYG (What You See Is What You Get) HTML editors available, such as Adobe PageMill, Claris Home Page, or GoLive CyberStudio. Just switch to their HTML Source modes, and script away. CyberStudio (currently available only for the Mac OS) even provides a built-in JavaScript creation and syntax checking feature (Figure 1.7).

2

Sᴛᴀʀᴛ Mᴇ Uᴘ!

Enough of the warm up; it's time to get
scripting. In this chapter, you'll learn where
to put your scripts in your HTML; how to
use alert boxes to communicate with the
user; how you can check for the presence
of browser plug-ins; and much more.
Let's get to it!

Where to put your scripts

Scripts can be put in either of two places on an HTML page: between the <HEAD> and </HEAD> tags (called a header script), or between the <BODY> and </BODY> tags (a body script). Script 2.1 is an example of a body script.

There is an HTML tag that denotes scripts, which, as you would guess, begins with <SCRIPT> and ends with </SCRIPT>.

To write your first script:

1. <SCRIPT>

Here's the opening script tag. This tells the browser to expect JavaScript instead of HTML.

2. document.write("Hello, world!")

Here's your first line of JavaScript: It takes the document window and writes "Hello, world!" into it, as seen in Figure 2.1.

3. </SCRIPT>

End writing JavaScript, and tell the browser to start expecting HTML again.

✔ Tips

■ For most of the rest of this book, we've left out the <SCRIPT> tags in our code explanations. As you'll see from the scripts themselves, they're still there and still needed, but we won't be cluttering our explanations with them.

■ You can have as many script tags (and therefore, multiple scripts) on a page as you'd like.

Script 2.1 Scripts always need to be enclosed inside the <SCRIPT> and </SCRIPT> HTML tags.

```
<HTML>
<HEAD>

<TITLE>My first script</TITLE>

</HEAD>
<BODY BGCOLOR=WHITE>
<H1><SCRIPT>

  document.write("Hello, world!")

</SCRIPT></H1>
</BODY>
</HTML>
```

Figure 2.1 The "Hello, world" example is de rigueur in code books. We'd probably lose our union card if we left it out.

Script 2.2 Here's how to shield your scripts from old browsers.

```
script

<HTML>
<HEAD>

<TITLE>My first script</TITLE>

</HEAD>
<BODY BGCOLOR=WHITE>
<H1><SCRIPT>
 <!-- Hide script from old browsers

 document.write("Hello, world!")

 // End hiding script from old browsers -->
</SCRIPT></H1>
</BODY>
</HTML>
```

Hiding scripts from old browsers

Older browsers, which include Netscape 1.x, Microsoft Internet Explorer versions 3 and earlier, and the America Online browser before version 4 don't understand JavaScript. While well-behaved browsers are supposed to ignore everything between tags they don't understand, not all of them do. There's a technique (as shown in Script 2.2) that will fool these backwards browsers into thinking that the contents of your script are actually HTML comments, which they will then ignore.

To hide JavaScript from old browsers:

1. `<!-- Hide script from old browsers`

   This line opens the HTML comment with the `<!--`.

2. `document.write("Hello, world!")`

   Here's the actual JavaScript, as in the previous example.

3. `// End hiding script from old browsers -->`

   This line starts with `//` which signifies a JavaScript comment, and ends with `-->` which ends an HTML comment.

✔ Tips

- This technique is used throughout this book, so we're only explaining it here. From now on, you should just assume that this is included.

- If you have a message that you want users of older browsers to see, you can add it into a `<NOSCRIPT>` tag. This will be processed both by badly behaved browsers, and by newer browsers when the user has (tragically) turned off JavaScript.

Putting comments in scripts

It's a good idea to get into the habit of adding comments to your scripts. You do this by inserting comments that JavaScript won't interpret as script commands. While your script may seem perfectly clear to you when you write it, if you come back to it a couple of months later it may seem as clear as mud. Comments will help to explain why you solved the problem in a particular way. Another reason to comment your script is to help other people who may want to re-use and modify your script.

The previous script showed an example of a single line comment, which is a line starting with //. Script 2.3 shows an example of a longer, multi-line comment.

To comment your script:

1. /* This is an example of a long JavaScript
→ comment. Note the characters at the
→ beginning and ending of the comment.
This script adds the words "Hello, world!"
→ into the body area of the HTML page.

The /* at the beginning of the line tells JavaScript to ignore everything that follows until it sees the end comment operator.

2. */

This is the end comment operator.

3. document.write("Hello, world!")

And here's the actual script again, as in the previous two examples. Yes, we're as tired of seeing this one as you are, but it's traditional for all code books to start off with the "Hello, world!" example.

So much for tradition.

Script 2.3 Here's how you can annotate your script with comments, helping you and others understand your code.

```
<HTML>
<HEAD>

<TITLE>My first script</TITLE>

</HEAD>
<BODY BGCOLOR=WHITE>
<H1><SCRIPT>
 <!-- Hide script from old browsers

 /* This is an example of a long JavaScript
   →comment. Note the characters at the
   →beginning and ending of the comment.

   This script adds the words "Hello, world!"
   →into the body area of the HTML page.
 */

 document.write("Hello, world!")

 // End hiding script from old browsers -->
</SCRIPT></H1>
</BODY>
```

Script 2.4 Alert dialog boxes help you communicate with the user.

```
<HTML>
<HEAD>

<TITLE>My JavaScript page</TITLE>
<SCRIPT LANGUAGE=JAVASCRIPT>
 <!-- Hide script from old browsers

 alert("Welcome to my JavaScript page!")

 // End hiding script from old browsers -->
</SCRIPT>

</HEAD>
<BODY BGCOLOR=WHITE>
<NOSCRIPT>
 <H2>This page requires JavaScript.</H2>
</NOSCRIPT>
</BODY>
</HTML>
```

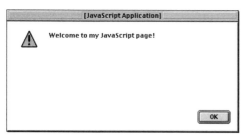

Figure 2.2 Although sometimes you don't have much to say.

Alerting the user

One of the main uses of JavaScript is to provide feedback to people browsing your site. You can create an alert window that will pop up and give the user the vitally important information that they need to know about your page.

In user interface design, less is generally more. For example, you could get the user's attention with loud alarm sirens and big animated banners, but that would be just a bit over the top. Instead, Script 2.4 shows how to create a nice, tasteful alert window. Now you know why the authors don't work for *Wired* magazine.

To alert a user:

1. alert("Welcome to my JavaScript page!")

   Yes, that's all there is to it, as shown in Figure 2.2. Just put the text that you want to have appear within the alert() method in quotes.

✔ Tips

- In JavaScript alert boxes, you'll always see text telling the user that the alert box was put up by a JavaScript command. It says "JavaScript Application" in Figure 2.2. This is a security feature to keep unscrupulous scripters from fooling hapless users. You can't code around this.

- You'll also see the <NOSCRIPT> tag used here. On non-JavaScript browsers (older browsers and browsers with JavaScript turned off), a message will appear saying that this page requires JavaScript.

ALERTING THE USER

Redirecting the user

Not only can you check for the existence of JavaScript, but you can also check for which version of JavaScript the user has (see Appendix A for more on JavaScript versions). Script 2.5 shows how to *redirect*, or send a user to another page, depending on which version of JavaScript their browser supports.

To redirect a user:

1. **<SCRIPT LANGUAGE=JAVASCRIPT1.1>**

   The LANGUAGE attribute to the SCRIPT tag lets you specify the minimum version of JavaScript the browser needs in order to run the script. In this case, the browser needs to have JavaScript 1.1 or later. If the user doesn't have a qualifying browser, they'll see a window like the one shown in Figure 2.3.

2. **window.location="intro4.html"**

   This line resets the location property of the current window. In other words, it tells the browser to change the current page to the specified page, in this case intro4.html.

3. **</SCRIPT>**

   The closing script tag.

✔ Tips

- There's no need to add a LANGUAGE attribute to the closing script tag.

- You can have different language versions on different scripts on one page. For example, one script might be for any JavaScript version, another for JavaScript 1.1 and higher, and a third for JavaScript 1.2.

- Unfortunately, there is no way to say that a script should apply to only JavaScript 1.1, for example. The language attribute will accept the specified version of JavaScript and higher.

Script 2.5 If the user has a JavaScript-capable browser, they'll be sent to a new page automatically.

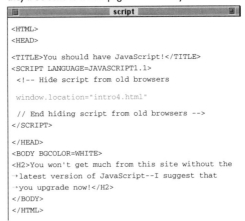

```
<HTML>
<HEAD>

<TITLE>You should have JavaScript!</TITLE>
<SCRIPT LANGUAGE=JAVASCRIPT1.1>
 <!-- Hide script from old browsers

 window.location="intro4.html"

 // End hiding script from old browsers -->
</SCRIPT>

</HEAD>
<BODY BGCOLOR=WHITE>
<H2>You won't get much from this site without the
→latest version of JavaScript--I suggest that
→you upgrade now!</H2>
</BODY>
</HTML>
```

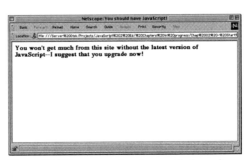

Figure 2.3 This message gives the user the heave-ho, if you've decided that JavaScript is essential to your site.

REDIRECTING THE USER

Script 2.6 You'll often want to check which browser a user has.

```
<HTML>
<HEAD>

<TITLE>What's your browser?</TITLE>

</HEAD>
<BODY BGCOLOR=WHITE>
<H2>
<SCRIPT LANGUAGE=JAVASCRIPT>
 <!-- Hide script from old browsers

 if (navigator.appName == "Netscape") {
   document.write("You're running Netscape
   →Navigator, a fine JavaScript-enabled
   →browser.")
 }
 else {
   document.write("You're not running Netscape
   →Navigator--maybe you should?")
 }

 // End hiding script from old browsers -->
</SCRIPT></H2>
</BODY>
</HTML>
```

Figure 2.4 If the user has Netscape, all is well.

Browser detection and conditionals

You'll often want to find out what browser the user has so that you can provide the most suitable page. This is called *browser detection*. Script 2.6 shows you how to check if the user is running Netscape. This script also introduces the idea of *conditionals*, which is where the script poses a test and performs different actions depending on the results of the test.

More about conditionals

Conditionals break down into three parts: the if section where we do our test, the *then* section, where we put the part of the script we want to do if the result is true, and an optional *else* section, which contains the part of the script we want to have happen if the result of the test is not true. The contents of what we're testing in the if section are in parentheses, and the contents of the other two sections are each contained in braces.

To discover the user's browser type (using a conditional):

1. if (navigator.appName=="Netscape") {

   This checks the appName (application name) property of the navigator object. If it is "Netscape," the script will continue on to the *then* part of the conditional. The opening brace { shows where the *then* part starts.

2. document.write("You're running Netscape → Navigator, a fine JavaScript-enabled → browser.")

   This write will only happen if the result of the above test is true, as shown in Figure 2.4. In other words, if appName isn't "Netscape," then this line won't be executed.

(Continued)

3. }

This closing brace ends the *then* part of the conditional.

4. else {

Because the *else* part of the conditional is optional, your script has to explicitly begin it. This is done by creating an *else* part with an opening brace.

5. document.write("You're not running Netscape
→ Navigator--maybe you should?")

This is the line that executes if appName isn't equal to "Netscape," as shown in Figure 2.5.

6. }

This closing brace ends the *else* part of the conditional.

✔ Tips

■ You can put as many statements as you wish inside the *then* and *else* braces.

■ The braces are not required on conditionals if (and only if) there is only one command in that part. For clarity's sake, we've always included the braces in the examples.

■ An alternate method of writing a conditional takes the form:
(condition) ? truePart : falsePart
which is the rough equivalent of:

```
if (condition) {
    truePart
}
else {
    falsePart
}
```

This book avoids this alternate syntax, again for clarity's sake, though you may see this format used in examples you find elsewhere. It makes your script much harder for others to follow.

Figure 2.5 If the user isn't running Netscape, then a mild admonishment is administered.

BROWSER DETECTION AND CONDITIONALS

Script 2.7 Testing for plug-ins will soon become second nature with a script like this.

```
                    script
<HTML>
<HEAD>

<TITLE>Got QuickTime?</TITLE>

</HEAD>
<BODY BGCOLOR=WHITE>
<H2>Here's tonight's dinner:<P>

<SCRIPT LANGUAGE=JAVASCRIPT>
 <!-- Hide script from old browsers

 if (navigator.plugins["QuickTime Plugin"]) {
   document.write("<embed src='images/dinner.mov'
   →width='160' height='144' loop='false'
   →autoplay='true'>")
 }
 else {
   document.write("<img src=images/dinner.gif
   →width='160' height='120'>")
 }

 // End hiding script from old browsers -->
</SCRIPT></H2>
</BODY>
</HTML>
```

Figure 2.6 If the user has QuickTime, then put the movie file on the page.

Figure 2.7 If QuickTime isn't present, replace the movie with a GIF.

Plug-in detection

Browser plug-ins provide the Web page author with lots of great options for including rich media content, such as sounds, video, and animation. The problem plug-ins pose is that you can't be sure if the user has the plug-ins installed that you require. JavaScript can help you find out what plug-ins the user has installed, and if they don't have what's needed, you can send them to a page where they can get the required plug-in. Script 2.7 tests for the presence of the QuickTime video plug-in, one of the most common.

To check for a plug-in:

1. if (navigator.plugins["QuickTime Plugin"]) {

   Because the script is posing a test, it uses a conditional if statement. In this case, it checks to see if the navigator.plugins object contains the name "QuickTime Plugin"; if so, the test returns a true result; i.e., the QuickTime plug-in is present.

2. document.write("<embed src='dinner.mov'
   → width='160' height='144' loop='false'
   → autoplay='true'>")
   }

   Because QuickTime is present, the script writes a bit of HTML to the document window. The <embed> tag is used for putting QuickTime movies into Web pages (Figure 2.6).

3. else {
   document.write("<img src='dinner.gif'
   → width='160' height='120'>")
   }

   Here's where the script deals with the possibility that QuickTime isn't available. If that's the case, a GIF image is substituted for the QuickTime movie (Figure 2.7).

Around and around with loops

In the last example, you checked to see if one particular plug-in was present. But if the user has multiple plug-ins (a very common occurrence), you're going to want to keep repeating the test until you check all of the plug-ins. To do this, you'll use a *loop*, which lets you repeat an action a specified number of times.

More about loops

The kind of loop used in this book is the for loop, named after the command that begins the loop. This sort of loop uses a *counter*, which is a variable that begins with one value (usually 0) and ends when a conditional test inside the loop is satisfied.

The for command which starts the loop structure is immediately followed by parentheses. Inside the parentheses you'll usually find the counter definition and the way the counter is incremented (i.e., the way the counter's value is increased). Script 2.8 shows you how to set up and use a loop to check all of a user's plug-ins for the presence of the Shockwave plug-in.

Script 2.8 Welcome to your first JavaScript loop.

```
<HTML>
<HEAD>

<TITLE>Got Shockwave?</TITLE>

</HEAD>
<BODY BGCOLOR=WHITE>
<H2>

<SCRIPT LANGUAGE=JAVASCRIPT>
 <!-- Hide script from old browsers

 hasShockwave = false
 for (i=0; i<navigator.plugins.length; i++) {
   if (navigator.plugins[i].name.indexOf
   →("Shockwave") >= 0) {
     hasShockwave = true
   }
 }

 if (hasShockwave) {
   document.write("You have Shockwave, you
   →lucky person, you!")
 }
 else {
   document.write("Sorry, you don't have
   →Shockwave.")
 }

 // End hiding script from old browsers -->
</SCRIPT></H2>
</BODY>
</HTML>
```

JavaScript Strings

When does a word like "cat" have a "t" in the 2nd position? When it's a JavaScript string.

In JavaScript, the first character is at position 0. So, using the example of "cat", "c" would be at position 0, "a" would be at position 1, and "t" would be in position 2.

Only when checking the length() of cat do we actually see a value of 3. All other string methods are zero-based, that is, they start with 0.

To use a loop to check for plug-ins:

1. hasShockwave = false

The first thing the script does is to set up a *boolean*, or logical, variable named hasShockwave. A boolean variable can only have the value true or false.

2. for (i=0; i<navigator.plugins.length; i++) {

This line begins the loop. The variable i is traditionally used by programmers to denote a variable used as a counter. First i is set to 0. A semicolon signals that there is another statement on the same line. The next part is read "if i is less than the number of plug-ins, then add 1 to the value of i." Because this is new, let's break that down a bit. The object navigator.plugins.length gives the number of installed plug-ins. The i++ part uses the ++ operator you saw in Chapter 1 to increment the value of i by 1.

3. if (navigator.plugins[i].name.
→ indexOf("Shockwave") >= 0) {

This line begins a conditional test inside the loop. The object navigator.plugins[i] uses the square brackets to indicate that the test should look at the plug-in on the list with the current value of i. So if the loop has already checked, say, two plug-ins, the value of i the next time through the loop would be 2 (JavaScript starts counting with 0, not 1; see the "JavaScript Strings" sidebar). The method indexOf() returns where (and if) the string "Shockwave" was found in navigator.plugins[i].name. If the string isn't found, the value is −1. If it is found, the value is its starting position (starting at 0 again).

(Continued)

4. hasShockwave = true

```
   }
}
```

When the test is satisfied, the hasShockwave variable gets set to true.

5. if (hasShockwave) {

This conditional test shows how things can be implied in JavaScript. This line can be read "If hasShockwave is true, go to the next step." In this case, having the variable within the parentheses of the if statement implies that the variable's value must be true to continue.

6. document.write("You have Shockwave, you ⇢ lucky person, you!")

```
}
```

If the test result is true, then write the text within the quotes to the document window (Figure 2.8).

7. else {
document.write("Sorry, you don't have ⇢ Shockwave.")

```
}
```

If the test failed, then give the sad news to the user with this statement.

Figure 2.8 After checking all of the plug-ins installed in the user's browser, the loop discovered that Shockwave was present.

Functions

Before you get into the next example, you need to learn about functions, which you'll use often when writing JavaScript. A *function* is a set of JavaScript statements that performs a task. Every function must be given a name, and can be invoked, or *called*, by other parts of the script.

Functions can be called as many times as needed during the running of the script. For example, let's say that you've gotten some information that a user typed into a form and you've saved it using JavaScript (there's more about this sort of thing in Chapter 5). If you need to use that information again and again, you could repeat the same code over and over in your script. But it's better to write that code once as a function, then call the function whenever you need it.

A function consists of the word function followed by the function name. There are always parentheses after the function name, followed by an opening brace. The statements that make up the function go on the following lines, then the function is closed by another brace. Here's what a function looks like:

```
function saySomething() {
    alert("Four score and seven years ago")
}
```

Notice that the line with alert is indented? That makes it easier to read your code. All of the statements between the first brace and the last one (and you probably noticed that those two lines are not indented) are part of the function.

Calling a function

You usually use an event handler to call a function. If you wanted to call the saySomething function when the user clicked a button, you would use code like this:

```
<INPUT TYPE="button" VALUE="Lincoln"
→ onClick="saySomething()"
```

Passing information to a function

You'll often want to take some information and give it to a function to be processed. This is called *passing* the information. Using the previous function example, the function is changed like this (and in Script 2.9):

```
function saySomething(message) {
    alert(message)
}
```

And the button code is also changed:

```
<INPUT TYPE="button" VALUE="Lincoln"
→ onClick="saySomething('Four score and
→ seven years ago...')">
```

The nice part about using this form is that you could have a bunch of buttons, and they could all call the same function, yet result in different alert messages, as seen in Figure 2.9.

```
<INPUT TYPE="button" VALUE="Lincoln"
→ onClick="saySomething('Four score and
→ seven years ago...')">
<INPUT TYPE="button" VALUE="Kennedy"
→ onClick="saySomething('Ask not what
→ your country can do for you...')">
<INPUT TYPE="button" VALUE="Nixon"
→ onClick="saySomething('I am not a
→ crook!')">
```

Script 2.9 You can call the same function again and again.

```
script

<HTML>
<HEAD>

<TITLE>Function passing</TITLE>

<SCRIPT LANGUAGE=JAVASCRIPT>
 <!-- Hide script from old browsers

 function saySomething(message) {
   alert(message)
 }

 // End hiding script from old browsers -->
</SCRIPT>
</HEAD>

<BODY BGCOLOR=WHITE>
<H2>
Famous Presidential Quotes
</H2>

<HR>
<FORM>
<INPUT TYPE="button" VALUE="Lincoln"
→onClick="saySomething('Four score and seven
→years ago...')">
<INPUT TYPE="button" VALUE="Kennedy"
→onClick="saySomething('Ask not what your
→country can do for you...')">
<INPUT TYPE="button" VALUE="Nixon"
→onClick="saySomething('I am not a crook!')">
</FORM>

</BODY>
</HTML>
```

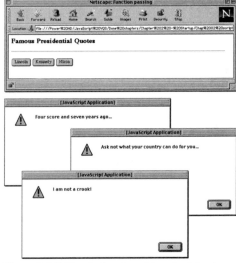

Figure 2.9 Calling the function with each of the three buttons in the top window results in three different responses, as shown in the three dialog boxes.

Script 2.10 Scrolling status messages aren't difficult to create.

```
<HTML>
<HEAD>

<TITLE>My JavaScript page</TITLE>
<SCRIPT LANGUAGE=JAVASCRIPT>
 <!-- Hide script from old browsers

 myMsg = "Hey, I know JavaScript - check out
 →my kewl scroller! ... "
 i=0

 function scrollMsg() {
   frontPart = myMsg.substring(i,myMsg.length)
   backPart = myMsg.substring(0,i)
   window.status = frontPart + backPart
   if (i < myMsg.length) {
     i++
   }
   else{
     i = 0
   }
   setTimeout("scrollMsg()",50)
 }
 // End hiding script from old browsers -->
</SCRIPT>

</HEAD>
<BODY BGCOLOR=WHITE onLoad="scrollMsg()">
<H2>I'm a kewl JavaScript dood with a scrolling
→status bar!</H2>
</BODY>
</HTML>
```

Figure 2.10 Note the message scrolling in the status bar at the bottom of this window.

Scrolling status bars

You've probably seen one of the most common JavaScript effects while you're surfing the Net. It's those messages that scroll in the status bar of browser windows. It's not especially difficult to do, and Script 2.10 shows you how. Figure 2.10 shows you the result; note the portion of the text in step 1 below at the bottom of the figure.

To make a scrolling status bar:

1. myMsg = "Hey, I know JavaScript - check → out my kewl scroller! ... "

This line sets the variable myMsg to the text within the quotes.

2. i=0

The variable i is traditionally used by programmers to denote a variable used as a counter. Throughout this script, i will increase in value and then be set back to zero, depending on what part of the script is executing. In this line, i is being initialized (or created) with an initial value of zero.

3. function scrollMsg() {

This line creates a function called scrollMsg.

4. frontPart = myMsg.substring(i,myMsg.length)

Here the first half of the scrolling message is set up by splitting myMsg into two parts. The method substring(x,y) acts on an object, in this case the string myMsg, and returns part of the string, starting with the character at x and stopping at one character before y. So, in this line, substring() is grabbing a part of myMsg, starting at i and ending at 56, which is one less than the number of characters in the string in step 1. This line sets frontPart to the right half of myMsg, starting at position i and continuing to the end of the string.

(Continued)

5. backPart = myMsg.substring(0,i)

This line sets backPart to the left half of myMsg, starting at position 0 and continuing up to position i. As i increases, frontPart gets progressively smaller and backPart gets progressively larger.

6. window.status = frontPart + backPart

This sets window.status, the status line property of the window object. In other words, it's the line at the bottom of your browser window that shows your current status. That area is immediately updated with the value of the variables frontPart and backPart, which were set in the previous steps. For example, if myMsg was "howdy," and i was 3, frontPart would be "dy" and backPart would be "how." Then, when i was incremented to 4, frontPart would be "y" and backPart would be "howd." Therefore, the status line would go from "dyhow" to "yhowd" to "howdy." Remember, JavaScript strings start with 0, not 1.

7. if (i < myMsg.length) {
   i++
}

If the value of i is less than the length of the variable myMsg, then add 1 to the value of i.

8. else{
   i = 0
}

If the value of i is the same or greater than myMsg, then set i back to zero.

You Have Been Warned

Scrolling status bars are widely considered to be a bit tasteless and a cliche these days, somewhat akin to the HTML <BLINK> tag (shudder). You might think twice before you add one of these to your sites.

9. setTimeout("scrollMsg()",50)
}

The setTimeout command is JavaScript's way of adding a pause to a process. Inside the parentheses, you put the name of the function you want to pause, add a comma to separate the name from the time period, then add the time period in milliseconds. In this line, you're applying setTimeout to the scrollMsg function. The length of the pause is 50 milliseconds. This will create a fairly fast scroll in the status bar.

✔ Tips

■ If you want the message to scroll faster, decrease the number "50" in step 9. To make the scroll slower, increase the number.

■ Chances are you don't deal with milliseconds in your daily life. Just remember that one second is equal to 1,000 milliseconds.

Status bar messages

Another trick you can do with the browser's status bar can be quite useful and effective: you can use the status bar to annotate a link, giving the user more information about the link when the cursor rolls over the link, but before the user clicks on the link. For example, if you have an image map on your page, you can use the status bar to describe the areas of the image map to the user. By giving the user more information, you enhance their experience with your site. Script 2.11 introduces a new way to use JavaScript: you can add JavaScript commands into HTML anchor tags (the tag used for links). Take a look at Figure 2.11 for the result.

To put a message in the status bar:

1. <A HREF="sean.html" onMouseOver=
   → "window.status='Best kid in the
   → world';return true">my son</A>

   This line is an HTML anchor tag with a standard text hyperlink in it, except for a snippet of JavaScript code. The onMouseOver event handler tells JavaScript to execute the action when the user moves the mouse pointer over the link. The action in this case is to set the window.status object (i.e., the message in the status bar) equal to the string 'Best kid in the world' when the user moves the pointer over the link my son. The ;return true is necessary to display the message; if it's not there, the message won't work.

2. <A HREF="cat.html" onMouseOver=
   → "window.status='A very cute cat'
   → ;return true">my cat</A>

   Proving an old Hollywood proverb wrong, this script manages to work well with both kids and animals. In this line the cat gets the same treatment as the kid in the preceding line.

Script 2.11 A rollover status message can be quite helpful to the user.

```
<HTML>
<HEAD>
<TITLE>Meaningful links</TITLE>
</HEAD>
<BODY BGCOLOR=WHITE>
<H1>Welcome to my page</H1>
<H2>
Click here to find out more about
→<A HREF="sean.html" onMouseOver="window.status=
→'Best kid in the world';return true">my son</A>,
or here to find out more about
→<A HREF="cat.html" onMouseOver="window.status=
→'A very cute cat';return true">my cat</A>.
</H2>
</BODY>
</HTML>
```

Figure 2.11 Note the custom status message for this link.

3

Fun with Images

One of the best uses of JavaScript is to add excitement to Web pages by animating graphics, and that's what this chapter is all about. Making images on Web pages change when the user moves the mouse over the image, thereby making the page react to the user, is one of the most common—and effective—tricks you can learn in JavaScript. This *rollover*, as it is called, is easy to implement, yet has many applications, as you'll see.

You can also use JavaScript to create images that change automatically, and even make animated advertising banners that take the place of animated GIF files.

Creating rollovers

The idea behind rollovers is simple. You have two images. The first, or *original* image is loaded and displayed along with the rest of the Web page by the user. When the user moves the mouse over the first image, the browser quickly swaps out the first image for the second, or *replacement* image, giving the illusion of movement or animation.

Script 3.1 gives you the bare-bones rollover; the whole thing is done within a standard image link. First a blue arrow is loaded (Figure 3.1), then it is overwritten when the user moves the mouse over the image by a red arrow that appears to the right of the blue arrow (Figure 3.2). The blue arrow is redrawn when the user moves the mouse away.

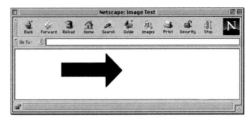

Figure 3.1 The first image, before the user moves the mouse over it.

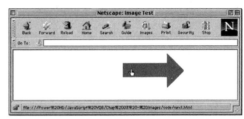

Figure 3.2 When the mouse is over the image, the script replaces the first image with the second image.

Script 3.1 Here's the simplest way to do a rollover, within a link tag.

```
                            script
<HTML>
<HEAD>
<TITLE>Image Test</TITLE>
</HEAD>

<BODY BGCOLOR="WHITE">
<CENTER>
<A HREF="next.html"
onmouseover="document.arrow.src='redArrow1.gif'"
onmouseout="document.arrow.src='blueArrow1.gif'">
<img src="blueArrow1.gif" width="300" height="82"
border="0" name="arrow"></A>
</CENTER></BODY></HTML>
```

Disadvantages to this kind of rollover

This method of doing rollovers is very simple, but you should be aware that there are some real problems with it.

■ Using this method will cause an error message in older browsers, such as Netscape 2.0 or earlier, Internet Explorer 3.0 or earlier, or the America Online 2.7 browser.

■ Because the second image is downloaded from the server at the time the user rolls over the first image, there can be a perceptible delay before the second image replaces the first one.

Rather than use this rollover method, we suggest that you use the following way of creating rollovers, which solves both problems.

To create a rollover:

1. `<A HREF="next.html"`

   The link begins by specifying where the browser will go when the user clicks on the image, in this case to the page next.html.

2. `onmouseover=`
   → `"document.arrow.src='redArrow1.gif'"`

   When the user moves the mouse over the image, the replacement image redArrow1.gif is written to the document window.

3. `onmouseout=`
   → `"document.arrow.src='blueArrow1.gif'">`

   Then, when the mouse moves away, the image blueArrow1.gif is swapped back in.

4. `<img src="blueArrow1.gif" width="300"`
   → `height="82" border="0"`
   → `name="arrow"></A>`

   The remainder of the image link defines the source of the original image for the page, and closes the link tag.

Creating more effective rollovers

To make the illusion of animation work, you need to make sure that the replacement image appears immediately, with no delay while it is fetched from the server. To do that, you use JavaScript to preload all the images into the browser's cache (so that they are already on the user's hard disk when they are needed) and place the images into script variables. Then when the user moves the mouse over an image, the script swaps out one variable containing an image for a second variable containing the replacement image. Script 3.2 shows how it is done. The visible result is the same as in Figures 3.1 and 3.2, but the apparent animation is smoother.

To create a better rollover:

1. if (document.images) {
    arrowRed = new Image
    arrowBlue = new Image
    arrowRed.src = 'redArrow1.gif'
    arrowBlue.src = 'blueArrow1.gif'
}

This code checks to see if the browser understands image objects (see sidebar). If the browser does, the code assigns arrowRed and arrowBlue to two separate image objects. Then, using the .src property, it fills the two objects with the GIFs of the red and blue arrows.

Script 3.2 This is a better way of doing rollovers than in Script 3.1, because it won't cause errors in older browsers and the animation is smoother.

```
<HTML>
<HEAD>

<TITLE>Image Test</TITLE>
<SCRIPT LANGUAGE=JAVASCRIPT>
  <!-- Hide script from old browsers

  if (document.images) {
    arrowRed = new Image
    arrowBlue = new Image

    arrowRed.src = 'redArrow1.gif'
    arrowBlue.src = 'blueArrow1.gif'
  }
  else {
    arrowRed = ""
    arrowBlue = ""
    document.arrow = ""
  }

  // End hiding script from old browsers -->
</SCRIPT>
</HEAD>
<BODY BGCOLOR="WHITE">
<CENTER><A HREF="next.html"
 onmouseover="document.arrow.src=arrowRed.src"
 onmouseout="document.arrow.src=arrowBlue.src">
<IMG SRC="blueArrow1.gif" WIDTH="300" HEIGHT="82"
BORDER="0" NAME="arrow"></A>
</CENTER></BODY>
</HTML>
```

A slick way to deal with the browser version problem

The bane of the HTML author (not to mention the JavaScript author) is making sure that the pages you create will work as intended on older browsers (or at least they won't look really horrible). One way to handle this problem would be to write code that checks for specific older browsers. You could write code that loops repeatedly and says to the browser "Are you Netscape 2? Are you Netscape 3? How about Internet Explorer 2.0?" and so on, stopping when it gets a positive answer. Trouble is, there are so many browser versions out there now that it's becoming difficult to make code like this work, especially as it becomes obsolete every time some company releases a new browser version.

Script 3.2 deals with this problem by checking **document.images**, which in effect says "Does the browser understand image objects?"

The trick here is that **document.images** is only implemented in JavaScript 1.1 and later, which was released with Netscape 3.0, and therefore eliminates a whole class of older browsers in one swoop.

2. else {
        arrowRed = ""
        arrowBlue = ""
        document.arrow = ""
    }

This is the code that tells old browsers (ones that failed the test in step 1) what to do. In order to keep from getting error messages in old browsers, we have to create some dummy variables—that is, variables that won't do anything but be created and set to empty. Think of them as placeholders. Create two variables named **arrowRed** and **arrowBlue**, and set them to empty. Then create and set **document.arrow** to empty, too.

3. <A HREF="next.html"
    → onmouseover=
    → "document.arrow.src=arrowRed.src"
    → onmouseout=
    → "document.arrow.src=arrowBlue.src">

The rest of the rollover gets handled in the link tag. When the user puts the mouse over the blue arrow graphic (onmouseover), the script swaps the blue arrow for the graphic with the red arrow (document.arrow.src=arrowRed.src). When the mouse cursor leaves the area of the graphic, the script reverts the graphic back to the blue arrow.

✔ Tip

■ When you prepare your graphics for rollovers, make sure that all your GIF images are *not* transparent. Transparent images will show the image they are replacing underneath.

Triggering rollovers from a link

In prior examples, the user triggered the rollover by moving the mouse over an image. But you can also make a rollover occur when the user points at a text link, as in Figures 3.3 and 3.4. All you need to do is to put a text link within the <A HREF tag, as in Script 3.3.

To trigger a rollover from a link:

1. <A HREF="next.html"
   → onmouseover=
   → "document.arrow.src=arrowRed.src"
   → onmouseout=
   → "document.arrow.src=arrowBlue.src">
   → <H1>Next page</H1></A>

   Note that the text link that says "Next page" is within the link tag, which makes it the thing that onmouseover and onmouseout use as a trigger. We've moved the IMG tag out of the link tag; it now follows the link tag.

✔ Tip

■ This trigger technique is useful when you want to provide the user with a preview of what they will see if they click the link at which they are pointing. For example, say you have a travel site describing trips to Scotland, Tahiti, and Cleveland. On the left of the page could be a column of text links for each destination, while on the right could be a preview area where an image appears. As the user points at the name of a destination, a picture of that place appears in the preview area. Clicking on the link takes the user to a page detailing their fabulous vacation spot.

Figure 3.3 The text link is the triggering device for this rollover.

Figure 3.4 When the user points at the link, the graphic below changes.

Script 3.3 This script triggers a rollover from a text link.

```
<HTML>
<HEAD>

<TITLE>Image Test</TITLE>
<SCRIPT LANGUAGE=JAVASCRIPT>
 <!-- Hide script from old browsers

 if (document.images) {
    arrowRed = new Image
    arrowBlue = new Image
    arrowRed.src = 'redArrow.gif'
    arrowBlue.src = 'blueArrow.gif'
 }
 else {
    arrowRed = ""
    arrowBlue = ""
    document.arrow = ""
 }
 // End hiding script from old browsers -->
</SCRIPT>
</HEAD>
<BODY BGCOLOR="WHITE">
<A HREF="next.html"
→ onmouseover="document.arrow.src=arrowRed.src"
→ onmouseout="document.arrow.src=arrowBlue.src">
→<H1>Next page</H1></A><BR>
<IMG SRC="blueArrow.gif" WIDTH="147" HEIGHT="82"
NAME="arrow">
</BODY>
</HTML>
```

Script 3.4 You can use JavaScript to cycle between images in a banner.

```
script

<HTML>
<HEAD>

<TITLE>Image Test</TITLE>
<SCRIPT LANGUAGE=JAVASCRIPT>
 <!-- Hide script from old browsers
 var adImages = new Array("banner1.gif",
 → "banner2.gif","banner3.gif")
 var thisAd = 0
 var imgCt = 3

 function cycle() {
   if (document.images) {
     thisAd++
     if (thisAd == imgCt) {
       thisAd = 0
     }
     document.adBanner.src=adImages[thisAd]
     setTimeout("cycle()", 3 * 1000)
   }
 }

 // End hiding script from old browsers -->
</SCRIPT>
</HEAD>
<BODY BGCOLOR=WHITE onload="cycle()">
<CENTER><IMG SRC="banner1.gif" WIDTH="400"
 →HEIGHT="75" NAME="adBanner"></CENTER>
</BODY>
</HTML>
```

Creating cycling banners

When you surf the Web, it's common to see advertising banners that periodically switch between images. Most of these are animated GIF files, which are GIF files that contain a number of frames which play in succession. If you want to have a page that cycles through a number of GIFs (either animated or not), you can use JavaScript to do the job, as in Script 3.4. This example uses three GIFs and cycles repeatedly through them.

To create cycling banners:

1. var adImages = new Array("banner1.gif",
   → "banner2.gif","banner3.gif")
   var thisAd = 0
   var imgCt = 3

   This code lays the foundation for the script by creating three variables. The first one, var adImages=new Array creates a new variable called adImages and fills it with a new kind of object, an *array*. An array is an object that contains a set of related information. In this case, the array contains the names of the three GIF files that make up the cycling banner. The two other variables, thisAd and imgCt, are given their beginning values in this code.

2. function cycle() {

   This line sets up a new function called cycle().

3. if (document.images) {

   Once again, you're checking to see if the browser understands the image object; if not, it's an old browser.

4. thisAd++

   Take the value of thisAd and add one to it.

(Continued)

5. if (thisAd == imgCt) {
        thisAd = 0

This code sets up a counter that says if the value of thisAd is equal to the value of imgCt, then set the value of thisAd back to zero.

6. document.adBanner.src=adImages[thisAd]

The image on the Web that is being cycled has the name adBanner; you define the name as part of the IMG tag, as shown in step 9. This line of code says that the source of the image adBanner is in the array adImages, and the value of the variable thisAd defines which of the three GIFs the browser should use at this moment.

7. setTimeout("cycle()", 3 * 1000)

This line tells the script how often to change GIFs in the banner. The command setTimeout lets you specify that an action should occur on a particular schedule, always measured in milliseconds. In this case, the function cycle is called every three thousand milliseconds, or every three seconds, so the GIFs will cycle in the banner every three seconds.

8. <BODY BGCOLOR=WHITE onload="cycle()">

In the BODY tag, you start the banner cycling by calling the cycle() function using the onload command.

9. <IMG SRC="banner1.gif" WIDTH="400"
    → HEIGHT="75" NAME="adBanner">

Here's where you define the name of the cycling image.

✔ Tip

- You might be wondering why you would want to use JavaScript for a cycling banner, rather than just create a animated GIF. One good reason is that it lets you use JPEGs in the banner, which gives you much higher quality images.

Figure 3.5 The first image, which starts the cycling banner …

Figure 3.6 … the second image …

Figure 3.7 … the final image.

CREATING CYCLING BANNERS

Script 3.5 You can delay the loading of the next image until the current one has finished loading.

```
script
<HTML>
<HEAD>

<TITLE>Image Test</TITLE>
<SCRIPT LANGUAGE=JAVASCRIPT>
 <!-- Hide script from old browsers
 var adImages = new Array("banner1.gif",
 →"banner2.gif","banner3.gif")
 var thisAd = 0

 function cycle() {
   if (document.images) {
     if (document.adBanner.complete) {
       thisAd++
       if (thisAd == 3) {
         thisAd = 0
       }
       document.adBanner.src=adImages[thisAd]
     }
     setTimeout("cycle()", 3 * 1000)
   }
 }

 // End hiding script from old browsers -->
</SCRIPT>
</HEAD>
<BODY BGCOLOR=WHITE onload="cycle()">
<CENTER><IMG SRC="banner1.gif" WIDTH="400"
→HEIGHT="75" NAME="adBanner"></CENTER>
</BODY>
</HTML>
```

Making the banner cycling wait for the user

If you're using small GIFs in your cycling banner, you probably won't have to worry that one GIF won't be done loading before the next one begins. But if you are using this technique for a slide show, you might want to make sure that the user has seen all of one graphic before starting the next—which is especially useful if the user has a slow Internet connection. Script 3.5 shows you how to vary your script to accomplish the goal. It is based on Script 3.4, but it adds another loop within the cycle function.

To make the cycling wait for the user:

1. if (document.adBanner.complete) {

   This line tells the document that the adBanner display must be complete.

2. thisAd++

   Add one to the value of the variable thisAd.

3. if (thisAd == 3) {
       thisAd = 0
       }

   When thisAd reaches the value 3, then set it back to zero.

4. document.adBanner.src=adImages[thisAd]
       }
   setTimeout("cycle()", 3 * 1000)

   This is similar to Script 3.4, except that this time the setTimeout command is outside the loop which governs the cycling of images. Not until that loop is complete will setTimeout be called.

Building slide shows

Slide shows on Web sites present the user with an image, and let the user control the progression (either forward or backward) of the images. JavaScript gives the user the interactive control needed. Script 3.6 shows how you can add slide shows to your pages.

To make a slide show:

1. var myPix = new Array("pathfinder.gif",
→ "surveyor.gif","surveyor98.gif")
    var thisPic = 0

You start out by declaring two variables, with myPix once again being an array with three GIF elements (there will be three images in this particular slide show). The thisPic variable will be used in a counter later in the script.

2. function processPrevious() {

Define a function called processPrevious. This moves the slide show backwards when the user clicks on the Previous link.

3. if (document.images && thisPic > 0) {
    thisPic--

If the document understands images and thisPic is greater than zero, then subtract one from the value of thisPic. The double ampersand is a logical operator meaning "and."

4. document.myPicture.src=myPix[thisPic]
    }
  }

Here you tell the document that the source of myPicture is found in the value of myPix, which is in turn dependent on the value of thisPic.

Script 3.6 This script builds a slide show.

```
<HTML>
<HEAD>

<TITLE>Image Test</TITLE>
<SCRIPT LANGUAGE=JAVASCRIPT>
 <!-- Hide script from old browsers
 var myPix = new Array("pathfinder.gif",
→"surveyor.gif","surveyor98.gif")
 var thisPic = 0

 function processPrevious() {
   if (document.images && thisPic > 0) {
     thisPic--
     document.myPicture.src=myPix[thisPic]
   }
 }

 function processNext() {
   if (document.images && thisPic < 2) {
     thisPic++
     document.myPicture.src=myPix[thisPic]
   }
 }

 // End hiding script from old browsers -->
</SCRIPT>
</HEAD>
<BODY BGCOLOR="WHITE">

<CENTER>
<H1>US Missions to Mars<p>
<IMG SRC="pathfinder.gif" NAME="myPicture"><p>
<A HREF=
→"javascript:processPrevious()>Previous</A> 
<A HREF=javascript:processNext()>Next</A>
</H1></CENTER></BODY>
</HTML>
```

Figure 3.8 When the Next link is clicked, the slide will advance. Note the javascript:processNext function shown in the status bar at the bottom of the window, which gives you feedback on what is happening.

Figure 3.9 The second image in the slide show.

Figure 3.10 Clicking the Previous link triggers the javascript:processPrevious function, as shown in the status bar.

5. function processNext() {
    if (document.images && thisPic < 2) {
        thisPic++
        document.myPicture.src=myPix[thisPic]
    }
}

This function is the mirror image of processPrevious. (Figure 3.8). This advances the images in the slide show by first checking if the value of thisPic is less than 2, and if so, by adding one to that value (Figures 3.9 and 3.10).

6. <IMG SRC="pathfinder.gif"
→ NAME="myPicture">

We have to define the value of myPicture in the script, and we do it in the IMG tag. This says that the initial source of the image is pathfinder.gif, but the generic name of the image for the purposes of the script is myPicture.

7. <A HREF=javascript:processPrevious()>
→ Previous</A>

Here's how you can call a JavaScript function from a link. When the user clicks on the Previous link, processPrevious is called.

8. <A HREF=javascript:processNext()>
→ Next</A>

The script calls the processNext function when the Next link is clicked.

✔ Tip

■ With both functions (processPrevious and processNext), when the user reaches the last image in either direction, the script ignores further clicks in that direction.

BUILDING SLIDE SHOWS

41

Displaying a random image

If your site is rich with graphics, or if you are displaying digital artwork, then you might want to have a random image from your collection appear when the user enters your site. Once again, JavaScript to the rescue! Script 3.7 is the answer.

To display a random image:

1. var myPix = new Array("mars.gif",
→ "jupiter.gif","saturn.jpg")

As is now familiar, build an array of images and stuff it into the variable myPix.

2. function choosePic() {

Define the function choosePic().

3. if (document.images) {
    randomNum =
    → Math.floor((Math.random() * 10)) % 3

If the document can handle image objects, then create a variable called randomNum. This variable gets the value of a math expression that's best read from the inside outwards. Math.random generates a random number between 0 and 1, which is then multiplied by 10. Math.floor rounds the result down to an integer, which means that the number must be between 0 and 9.

Script 3.7 An array can help you display random images when a user loads the page, adding variety and a sense of surprise to your site.

```
                          script
<HTML>
<HEAD>

<TITLE>Image Test</TITLE>
<SCRIPT LANGUAGE=JAVASCRIPT>
 <!-- Hide script from old browsers
 var myPix = new Array("mars.gif","jupiter.gif",
→"saturn.jpg")

 function choosePic() {
   if (document.images) {
     randomNum =
→Math.floor((Math.random() * 10)) % 3
     document.myPicture.src = myPix[randomNum]
   }
 }

 // End hiding script from old browsers -->
</SCRIPT>
</HEAD>
<BODY BGCOLOR="WHITE" onload="choosePic()">
<IMG SRC="spacer.gif" WIDTH="200" HEIGHT="200"
→NAME="myPicture"><p>
</BODY>
</HTML>
```

The percentage sign % is the JavaScript operator for modulus. In case you've forgotten your high school algebra, that means that you take the first number and divide it by the second number. The modulus is the remainder. Any number from 0 to 9 modulo 3 will be either 0, 1 or 2; i.e., if you divide any number from 0 to 9 by 3, the integer part of the remainder will be either 0, 1, or 2.

4. document.myPicture.src =
→ myPix[randomNum]
     }
   }

This says that the source of the image myPicture is found in the variable myPix, and the value at this moment is dependent on the value of randomNum.

5. <BODY BGCOLOR="WHITE"
→ onload="choosePic()">

We use the onload command to start the choosePic function.

6. <IMG SRC="spacer.gif" WIDTH="200"
→ HEIGHT="200" NAME="myPicture">

The image displayed gets the name myPicture, so you can use the script to change the image.

Combining a rollover with an image map

You're probably familiar with image maps in regular HTML, where you can click on a part of a graphic that has hot spots on it, and depending on which hot spot you click, you'll go to a different page. For example, if you have a map of the United States, each state could have its own hot spot. Clicking on a state brings you to a page with detailed information about that state.

Combining rollovers with an image map can give you some extremely interesting and attractive results. Find out how to master this technique in Script 3.8.

Before you look at the script, check out Figures 3.11, 3.12, 3.13, and 3.14 to see how rollovers and image maps work together. As you'll note, there's one big graphic called Book Info, with three sub-areas that become visible when the user rolls the mouse over them.

To combine a rollover with an image map:

1. if (document.images) {
       img1 = new Image
       img2 = new Image
       img3 = new Image
       imgBlue = new Image
       imgRed = new Image

   Do a quick test to see if the user's browser can handle the level of JavaScript you're using with the document.images test. If all's well, create five new image objects.

   (Continued)

Figure 3.11 The "Book Info" image is actually an image map.

Figure 3.12 Pointing at the top third of the image map changes the image to "reveal" a new interface choice.

Figure 3.13 Revealing the second choice.

Figure 3.14 The third choice. Each choice, when clicked, takes you to a different page.

Script 3.8 Combining image maps and rollovers is a powerful technique that adds interest and movement to your sites.

```
script
<HTML>
<HEAD>
 <TITLE>Combining rollovers &amp; image maps</TITLE>
<SCRIPT LANGUAGE=JAVASCRIPT><!-- Hide script from old browsers
 if (document.images) {
   img1 = new Image
   img2 = new Image
   img3 = new Image
   imgBlue = new Image
   imgRed = new Image

   img1.src = "testGreen1.gif"
   img2.src = "testGreen2.gif"
   img3.src = "testGreen3.gif"
   imgBlue.src = "testBlue.gif"
   imgRed.src = "testRed.gif"
 }
 else {
   img1 = ""
   img2 = ""
   img3 = ""
   imgBlue = ""
   imgRed = ""
   document.roll = ""
 }

 // End hiding script from old browsers --></SCRIPT>
</HEAD>
<BODY BGCOLOR=WHITE>

<P><TABLE BORDER=0>
 <TR>
   <TD WIDTH="132">
     <P><A HREF="home.html" onmouseover="document.roll.src=imgBlue.src"
→ onmouseout="document.roll.src=imgRed.src">
     <MAP NAME="roll_test">
       <AREA SHAPE=RECT COORDS="0,0,120,60" HREF="sec1.HTML" onmouseover="document.roll.src=img1.src">
       <AREA SHAPE=RECT COORDS="0,60,120,120" HREF="sec2.HTML" onmouseover="document.roll.src=img2.src">
       <AREA SHAPE=RECT COORDS="0,120,120,180" HREF="sec3.HTML" onmouseover="document.roll.src=img3.src">
     </MAP>
     <IMG USEMAP="#roll_test" SRC="testRed.gif" WIDTH=120 HEIGHT=180 BORDER=0 ALIGN=bottom name=roll></A>
   </TD><TD VALIGN=top>
     <H3>Thanks for visiting our site. You'll find some of the
     best JavaScript information on the Web right here, much of
     which we also put into our book, JavaScript for the World
     Wide Web, Visual QuickStart Guide, Second Edition, published
     by Peachpit Press. You can find out more by clicking on the
     info box to the left.</H3>
   </TD></TR>
</TABLE></P>
</BODY>
</HTML>
```

2.
```
    img1.src = "testGreen1.gif"
    img2.src = "testGreen2.gif"
    img3.src = "testGreen3.gif"
    imgBlue.src = "testBlue.gif"
    imgRed.src = "testRed.gif"
}
```
Fill the new image objects with their initial source images.

3.
```
else {
    img1 = ""
    img2 = ""
    img3 = ""
    imgBlue = ""
    imgRed = ""
    document.roll = ""
}
```
If the test for a modern browser failed, fill the variables with null values so that you don't get an error message from the old browser.

4.
```
<A HREF="home.html"
→ onmouseover=
→ "document.roll.src=imgBlue.src"
→ onmouseout=
→ "document.roll.src=imgRed.src">
```
Here you're opening the link tag and defining the beginning values for the onmouseover and onmouseout.

5.
```
<MAP NAME="roll_test">
```
This is where you give the image map a name.

6. `<AREA SHAPE=RECT`
→ `COORDS="0,0,120,60"`
→ `HREF="sec1.HTML"`
→ `onmouseover=`
→ `"document.roll.src=img1.src">`

`<AREA SHAPE=RECT`
→ `COORDS="0,60,120,120"`
→ `HREF="sec2.HTML"`
→ `onmouseover=`
→ `"document.roll.src=img2.src">`

`<AREA SHAPE=RECT`
→ `COORDS="0,120,120,180"`
→ `HREF="sec3.HTML"`
→ `onmouseover=`
→ `"document.roll.src=img3.src">`

In these lines of code, you define the shape and size of the three rectangular hot spots on the image map, and for each one, tell the script that onmouseover, it should assign the appropriate source to the document.roll.src object.

7. `</MAP>`
`<IMG USEMAP="#roll_test"`
→ `SRC="testRed.gif" WIDTH=120`
→ `HEIGHT=180 BORDER=0`
→ `ALIGN=bottom name=roll></A>`

You've finished defining the image map, so close the map tag and name the map in the IMG tag, use testRed.gif as the initial image, and name the image roll. Finally, close the link tag with </A>.

✔ Tips

■ Each section of the map links to a different Web page. The browser doesn't go to a new Web page until the user clicks the mouse.

■ This technique is terrific for helping to unclutter crowded layouts and navigation bars. In effect, it lets you layer your user interfaces.

COMBINING A ROLLOVER WITH AN IMAGE MAP

Automatically changing background colors

To be honest, we're not exactly sure why you would want to change your page's background colors with JavaScript, but since you can do it, we figured we would let you in on the technique. In Figures 3.15 and 3.16, you can see how we're changing the background color every three seconds, cycling between red, white, and blue (not shown). Get the lowdown on how to do it in Script 3.9.

To automatically change background colors:

1. var bGrounds =
→ new Array("red","white","blue")
var thisBG = 0
var bgColorCount = 3

The bGrounds variable contains the names of the colors you will use. You could use hex colors here with no problems; you can even mix and match hex with color names. The thisBG variable gets set to zero, and the variable bgColorCount gets set to 3.

2. function rotateBG() {

Define a function called rotateBG.

3. if (document.images) {
thisBG++

If the document knows how to handle images, then increment the value of thisBG by one.

Figure 3.15 The initial white background.

Figure 3.16 The same page, now with a red background.

Script 3.9 This script lets your page change backgrounds automatically.

```
                    script
<HTML>
<HEAD>

<TITLE>Image Test</TITLE>
<SCRIPT LANGUAGE=JAVASCRIPT>
 <!-- Hide script from old browsers
 var bGrounds = new Array("red","white","blue")
 var thisBG = 0
 var bgColorCount = 3

 function rotateBG() {
   if (document.images) {
     thisBG++
     if (thisBG == bgColorCount) {
       thisBG = 0
     }
     document.bgColor=bGrounds[thisBG]
     setTimeout("rotateBG()", 3 * 1000)
   }
 }

 // End hiding script from old browsers -->
</SCRIPT>
<HEAD>
<BODY BGCOLOR="RED" onload="rotateBG()">
<P>
<CENTER><H1>Welcome to Steve's<BR> Wacko Internet
→Conspiracy Page!</H1>
</CENTER>
<P><H3>Have you ever felt that people out there
→were out to get you? Well, we feel that way too,
→and we think we know why they're out to get you,
→too. Assassinations, secret world-government
→takeovers, crop circles, frogs falling from the
→sky, black helicopters... we've got the REAL
→story behind them all.</H3></P>
<CENTER><H1>The truth is in here. Somewhere.</H1>
</CENTER></BODY>
</HTML>
```

4. if (thisBG == bgColorCount) {
    thisBG = 0
    }

If thisBG is equal to bgColorCount, then set thisBG back to zero. Otherwise, it proceeds back through the loop!

5. document.bgColor=bGrounds[thisBG]

This line tells the document to set its background color property to the value represented by the variable bGrounds, which is determined by the current value of thisBG.

6. setTimeout("rotateBG()", 3 * 1000)
    }
    }

As seen earlier in this chapter, setTimeout calls the rotateBG function every 3000 milliseconds.

✔ Tips

- You could have the script switch between more colors by adding more color names or hex values to the bGrounds array, and adjusting the number assigned to bgColorCount to match the number of colors

- For that retro psychedelic effect, you can get the colors to flash really quickly by decreasing the setTimeout value. If you change the value 3 in step 6 to a small value like .1, you'll think you're re-experiencing the Sixties in no time.

FRAMES, FRAMES, AND MORE FRAMES

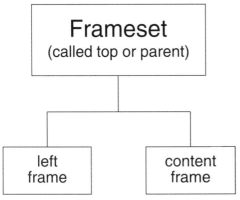

Figure 4.1 Layout of a frameset that contains two frames, "left" and "content."

Frames are one of the most powerful features of HTML. In this chapter, we'll show how to harness the power of JavaScript to make frames even more powerful.

A frame consists of at least three pages of HTML. The first, called the *frameset*, sets up the dimensions of each of the child frames. The frameset is referred to in JavaScript as top or parent. The remainder of the pages fit into the panes that the frameset has created, and are the child pages. These can be named anything you choose. Figure 4.1 shows a frameset that creates two child frames, "left" and "content."

Keeping a page out of a frame

Other people can put one of your pages inside a frame on their site, making it appear that your page is part of their content. In JavaScript, windows appear in a hierarchy, with the parent window at the top of the heap. When someone hijacks your page, they are forcing it to be a child frame to their parent window. Figure 4.2 shows how the page would appear as part of someone else's site. With Script 4.1, you can prevent this page hijacking and force your page to always be in a browser window by itself

To isolate your page:

1. if (top.location != self.location) {

First, check to see if the location of the current page (self) is the top-most in the browser window hierarchy. If it is, there's no need to do anything.

2. top.location = self.location
}

If the current page isn't at the top, set the top to be the current page. This will force the current window to be your page and your page only. Figure 4.3 shows your page, as you designed it.

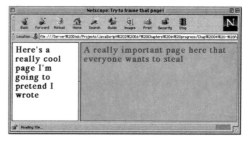

Figure 4.2 Your page, buried in someone else's frameset.

Script 4.1 JavaScript provides a way to force your page to always appear on a separate page.

```
<HTML>
<HEAD>

<TITLE>Can't be in a frame</TITLE>
<SCRIPT LANGUAGE=JAVASCRIPT>
 <!-- Hide script from old browsers
 if (top.location != self.location) {
    top.location = self.location
 }
 // End hiding script from old browsers -->
</SCRIPT>

</HEAD>
<BODY BGCOLOR=WHITE>
<H1>A really important page here that everyone
→wants to steal</H1>
</BODY>
</HTML>
```

Figure 4.3 Your page, after escaping from the evil hijacking frameset.

Script 4.2 Use JavaScript to force your page into a frameset.

```
script
<HTML>
<HEAD>

<TITLE>Must be in a frame</TITLE>
<SCRIPT LANGUAGE=JAVASCRIPT>
 <!-- Hide script from old browsers
 if (top.location == self.location) {
   top.location.href = "frameset2.html"
 }
 // End hiding script from old browsers -->
</SCRIPT>

</HEAD>
<BODY BGCOLOR=WHITE>
<H1>A page that should always be within a
→frame</H1>
</BODY>
</HTML>
```

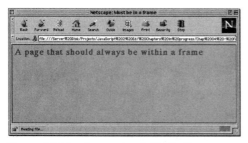

Figure 4.4 A lonely page, stranded by itself.

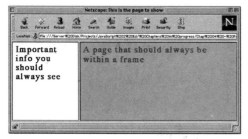

Figure 4.5 Your page, happily reunited with its parent and sibling.

Forcing a page into a frame

When a search engine catalogs one of your pages, it doesn't know that the page is part of a frame. When a user finds your page via the search engine, clicking on the link will show just the single page, not the full frameset as you designed it. Script 4.2 shows you how to force the full frameset to display even though AltaVista or another search engine doesn't know about the frameset. Figure 4.4 shows the page looking out-of-place, and Figure 4.5 shows it at home, snug in its frame.

To force a frame:

1. if (top.location == self.location) {

   Check to see if the current page (self) is at the top-most level. If it isn't, you're in a frameset.

2. top.location.href="frameset2.html"
   }

   If the location of the current page is at the top, then replace the current page with the URL of the frameset. This will then display your framed site as you designed it.

Loading a frame

It's common to have one frame that serves as a navigation bar for your site, which loads the different pages into the main frame. In Script 4.3 you load your choice of page into the main content frame, just by clicking on a link in the left frame.

To load one frame from another:

1. pageArray = new Array ("", "frame3a.html",
   → "frame3b.html", "frame3c.html")

   Create a new array called pageArray, which contains the URLs available from the navigation bar. In the page shown in Figure 4.6, there are three possible pages that can be displayed in the content frame, so you need three URLs. The first position in the array is position 0, which we leave blank so that we can use positions 1, 2, and 3 of the array to match pages 1, 2, and 3.

2. function setContent(thisPage) {
   parent.content.document.location.href =
   → pageArray[thisPage]
   }

   Create a new function called setContent, which, when given a page number, loads the content frame with the requested page. It does this by finding the parent of the current document, then finding the content frame of the parent document, and then loading the new page into that frame by setting the location.href, the URL source, for that frame document.

3. <A HREF = "javascript:setContent(1)">
   → Page 1</A>

   Within the body of the page, create links to pages that you want loaded into the main window. When the link is clicked, the JavaScript function setContent is called and passed the page number (1, in this case) that we want to load. Repeat this line, with a new page number, for each page that you want to show in the content frame.

Script 4.3 Use this script to set up the content from the navigation frame.

```
script
<HTML>
<HEAD>
<TITLE>Nav Bar</TITLE>
<SCRIPT LANGUAGE=JAVASCRIPT>
 <!-- Hide script from old browsers
 pageArray = new Array ("","frame3a.html",
 →"frame3b.html","frame3c.html")

 function setContent(thisPage) {
   parent.content.document.location.href =
   →pageArray[thisPage]
 }
 // End hiding script from old browsers -->
</SCRIPT>

</HEAD>

<BODY BGCOLOR=WHITE>
<H1>Navigation Bar</H1>
<H2>
<A HREF="javascript:setContent(1)">Page 1</A><BR>
<A HREF="javascript:setContent(2)">Page 2</A><BR>
<A HREF="javascript:setContent(3)">Page 3</A>
</H2>
</BODY>
</HTML>
```

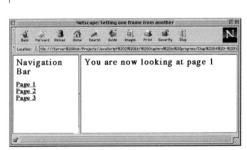

Figure 4.6 Here's a frame acting as a navigation bar with the content page appearing in a content frame."

Script 4.4 JavaScript lets you create the HTML on-the-fly, writing new pages as the result of a script.

```
                    script
<HTML>
<HEAD>
<TITLE>Nav Bar</TITLE>
<SCRIPT LANGUAGE=JAVASCRIPT>
 <!-- Hide script from old browsers
 function writeContent(thisPage) {
   parent.content.document.write
 → ("<HTML><HEAD></HEAD>
 →<BODY BGCOLOR=WHITE><H1>")
   parent.content.document.write("You are now
 →looking at page "+thisPage+".")
   parent.content.document.write
 → ("</H1></BODY></HTML>")
   parent.content.document.close()
 }
 // End hiding script from old browsers -->
</SCRIPT>

</HEAD>

<BODY BGCOLOR=WHITE>
<H1>Navigation Bar</H1>
<H2>
<A HREF="javascript:writeContent(1)">
→Page 1</A><BR>
<A HREF="javascript:writeContent(2)">
→Page 2</A><BR>
<A HREF="javascript:writeContent(3)">
→Page 3</A>
</H2>
</BODY>
</HTML>
```

Figure 4.7 And here's the result, a web page written by a JavaScript.

Creating and loading a dynamic frame

Because JavaScript can create page content on-the-fly, it's useful for loading dynamic data into frames based on a user's choice in another frame. Script 4.4 creates a page and loads it into the main content frame.

To load a dynamic frame from another frame:

1. function writeContent(thisPage) {
   parent.content.document.write
   → ("<HTML><HEAD></HEAD>
   → <BODY BGCOLOR=WHITE><H1>")
   parent.content.document.write
   → ("You are now looking at page
   → "+thisPage+".")
   parent.content.document.write
   → ("</H1></BODY></HTML>")
   parent.content.document.close()
   }

   Create a new function called writeContent, which, when given a page number, creates a dynamic page and then loads it into the content frame. It does this by finding the parent of the current document, then finding the content frame of the parent document, and then writing the new page into the content document. We finish with document.close() to make sure that everything we've written is displayed.

2. <A HREF = "javascript:writeContent(1)">
   → Page 1</A>

   Within the body of the page, create links to pages that you want loaded into the main window. When the link is clicked, the JavaScript function writeContent is called and passed the page number (1, in this case) that we want to create and load. Figure 4.7 shows the result. Repeat this line, with a new page number, for each page that you want to create and show in the content frame.

Sharing functions between frames

One common frame layout is to use a permanent navigation frame and a content page that might have a variety of different pages. If all those content pages need to call an identical JavaScript, it makes sense to put the function into the page that's always present instead of duplicating it for every possible content page. In Figure 4.8, we use this capability to have many pages share an identical function that returns a selected banner image. This will require that part of the code be in the navigation frame and part in the content frame.

To use a function on another page:

1. function setBanner() {

In Script 4.5, which is in the navigation frame, we create a new function called setBanner.

2. if (document.images) {

We check to see if this browser supports the images object. If it doesn't, executing the next line would cause an error.

3. bannerImg = new Image
bannerImg.src = 'blueBanner.gif'

Create a new image named **bannerImg** and set its source to be the URL of the selected image. Changing the value of this variable, or using one of the random image routines from Chapter 3, will change the banner for every page that calls this function.

Script 4.5 Write a JavaScript function once and use it on many pages to set up the image of the day.

```
<HTML>
<HEAD>
<TITLE>Nav Bar</TITLE>
<SCRIPT LANGUAGE=JAVSCRIPT>
 <!-- Hide script from old browsers
 function setBanner() {
   if (document.images) {
     bannerImg = new Image
     bannerImg.src = 'blueBanner.gif'
     return (bannerImg.src)
   }
   return ("")
 }
 // End hiding script from old browsers -->
</SCRIPT>

</HEAD>

<BODY BGCOLOR=WHITE>
<H1>Navigation Bar</H1>
<H2>
<A HREF="frame5a.html" target=content>
→Page 1</A><BR>
<A HREF="frame5b.html" target=content>
→Page 2</A><BR>
<A HREF="frame5c.html" target=content>
→Page 3</A>
</H2>
</BODY>
</HTML>
```

Script 4.6 Call the common JavaScript function in the navigation frame to display the image of the day.

```
<HTML>
<HEAD>

<TITLE>Content Frame</TITLE>

</HEAD>
<BODY BGCOLOR=WHITE>
<CENTER>Today's Featured site:<BR>
<IMG SRC=spacer.gif WIDTH=400 HEIGHT=75
→NAME=adBanner>
<SCRIPT LANGUAGE=JAVASCRIPT>
  <!-- Hide script from old browsers

  document.adBanner.src = parent.left.setBanner()

  // End hiding script from old browsers -->
</SCRIPT>
</CENTER><H1>You are now looking at page 1</H1>
</BODY>
</HTML>
```

Figure 4.8 And here's the result of the two scripts.

4. return (bannerImg.src)
}
Return the value of the new banner you've set.

5. return ("")
}
The script will only reach this line when the browser is too old to understand the images object. So, the script returns an empty string instead of an image.

6. document.adBanner.src =
→ parent.left.setBanner()
Script 4.6, which is in the content frame, sets the local variable **adBanner** to be the new banner image returned by **setBanner** in parent.left (the navigation frame).

SHARING FUNCTIONS BETWEEN FRAMES

Storing information in frames

In situations similar to that in the previous example, you can also keep track of useful information across frames, by storing the variables in the permanent frame page. Figure 4.9 shows how many times a user has visited each content page this session. Once again, scripts are needed in multiple frames.

To keep a count of page visits:

1. page1Count = 0
   page2Count = 0
   page3Count = 0

   In Script 4.7, in the navigation frame, we initialize the three variables we want to keep track of, one for each content page.

2. parent.left.page1Count++

   In the header area of Script 4.8, in the content frame, we add one to the counter page1Count, located in the navigation frame. Use a different counter variable for each content page.

3. document.write(parent.left.page1Count)

   In the body area of Script 4.8, you use the page1Count variable, which displays the number of times that a visitor has visited this page in this session.

Figure 4.9 The JavaScript says that you have viewed Page 2 three times in this session.

Script 4.7 Initialize the JavaScript variables in the navigation frame.

```
<HTML>
<HEAD>
<TITLE>Nav Bar</TITLE>
<SCRIPT LANGUAGE=JAVASCRIPT>
 <!-- Hide script from old browsers
 page1Count = 0
 page2Count = 0
 page3Count = 0

 pageArray = new Array ("","frame6a.html",
 →"frame6b.html","frame6c.html")

 function setContent(thisPage) {
   parent.content.document.location.href =
   →pageArray[thisPage]
 }

 // End hiding script from old browsers -->
</SCRIPT>

</HEAD>

<BODY BGCOLOR=WHITE>
<H1>Navigation Bar</H1>
<H2>
<A HREF="javascript:setContent(1)">Page 1</A><BR>
<A HREF="javascript:setContent(2)">Page 2</A><BR>
<A HREF="javascript:setContent(3)">Page 3</A>
</H2>
</BODY>
</HTML>
```

Script 4.8 Add one to the JavaScript page counter and and show the result.

```
<HTML>
<HEAD>

<TITLE>Show page counter</TITLE>
<SCRIPT LANGUAGE=JAVASCRIPT>
 <!-- Hide script from old browsers

 parent.left.page1Count++

 // End hiding script from old browsers -->
</SCRIPT>

</HEAD>
<BODY BGCOLOR=WHITE>
<H1>You are now looking at page 1.</H1>
<H2>You have been to this page
<SCRIPT LANGUAGE=JAVASCRIPT>
 <!-- Hide script from old browsers
 document.write(parent.left.page1Count)

 // End hiding script from old browsers -->
</SCRIPT>
times.</H2>
</BODY>
</HTML>
```

STORING INFORMATION IN FRAMES

VERIFYING FORMS

Figure 5.1 This example form might appear on a car dealer's Web site.

Any time you need to gather information from the users of your Web sites, you'll need to use a form.

Forms can contain most of the usual graphical interface elements including entry fields, radio buttons, check boxes, pop-up menus, and entry lists. In addition, HTML forms can contain password fields, shielding the user's input from prying eyes.

Once the form is filled out, a click on the form's Submit button sends the form's information to your Web server, where a CGI (that stands for Common Gateway Interface, and it's a script that runs on the Web server) interprets the data and acts on it. Often, the data is then stored in a database for later use. It's useful to make sure that the data the user enters is "clean," that is, accurate and in the correct format, before it gets stored on the server side. JavaScript is the perfect way to check the data; this is called *form validation*. Though the CGI can do the validation, it's much faster and more efficient to do it on the client's machine with JavaScript.

In this chapter, you'll learn how to use JavaScript to make sure that your forms contain valid information, how to check data in one field against the data in another field, and how you can highlight incorrect information to let the user know what needs to be changed.

Validating Email addresses

Internet addresses can be tricky things for users, especially new users, to type. You can help them out by scanning the e-mail address they enter and checking it for improper form. For example, you can check that there's only one @ sign, and that there are no invalid characters, as there are in Figure 5.2. The limit, of course, is that your script can't catch mispellings, so if the user meant to type in joe@myprovider.com and instead entered joe@yprovider.com the mistake will go through. Script 5.1 shows you how to snoop through an address for errors.

To validate an Email address:

1. function validEmail(email) {

   First define a function to which the contents of the email field on the form are passed.

2. invalidChars = " /:,;"

   Create a variable, invalidChars, that contains the five invalid characters for an email address: blank space, slash, colon, comma, and semicolon.

3. if (email == "") {
   return false
   }

   This test says "If the contents of email is nothing, then the result is false."

4. for (i=0; i<invalidChars.length; i++) {

   In this for statement, start a loop that scans through the invalidChars string. Start by initializing the counter i to zero, then each time through the loop that i is less than the length of the string, add 1 to i with the i++ increment operator.

Figure 5.2 Here's an example of the kind of entry error that the validation script will catch.

Script 5.1 By scanning through the text within an email field on your form, you can ensure that you get proper email addresses.

```
<SCRIPT LANGUAGE="JavaScript">
 <!-- Hide script from older browsers
 function validEmail(email) {
    invalidChars = " /:,;"
    if (email == "") {
      return false
    }
    for (i=0; i<invalidChars.length; i++) {
      badChar = invalidChars.charAt(i)
      if (email.indexOf(badChar,0) != -1) {
        return false
      }
    }
    atPos = email.indexOf("@",1)
    if (atPos == -1) {
      return false
    }
    if (email.indexOf("@",atPos+1) != -1) {
      return false
    }
    periodPos = email.indexOf(".",atPos)
    if (periodPos == -1) {
      return false
    }
    if (periodPos+3 > email.length) {
      return false
    }
    return true
 }
 function submitIt(form) {
    if (!validEmail(form.emailAddr.value)) {
      alert("Invalid email address")
      form.emailAddr.focus()
      form.emailAddr.select()
      return false
    }
    return true
 }
 // End hiding script -->
</SCRIPT>
```

VALIDATING EMAIL ADDRESSES

About These Scripts

The script examples in this chapter are in fact snippets from a complete form script named "Car Picker."

You can see the entire script in Script 5.8 on pages 70 through 72 at the end of this chapter.

5. badChar = invalidChars.charAt(i)
    if (email.indexOf(badChar,0) != –1) {
       return false
    }
}

The badChar variable saves the position of the invalid character in the invalidChars string. For example, if the invalid character was a colon, badChar would contain 2, the position of the colon in the five-character string (remember that JavaScript starts numbering at 0). indexOf looks for the position of a character in a string. If the result of the indexOf function is –1, the character isn't in the string, and you again get a false result.

6. atPos = email.indexOf("@",1)
if (atPos == -1) {
    return false
}

The atPos variable holds the position of the @ sign. Using indexOf, the script checks for the first @ sign, starting at the second character in the address. If the result is that the position of the @ sign is –1, it means that there is no @ sign in the address, and you've got trouble in Address City.

7. if (email.indexOf("@",atPos+1) != –1) {
    return false
}

Now the script is making sure that there is only one "@" sign, and rejecting anything with more than one "@", by checking characters beginning at 1 character past where we found the first "@". The exclamation point means "not," so if there's an "@" sign in any position that is not –1, then the string fails the test.

(Continued)

8. periodPos = email.indexOf(".",atPos)
   if (periodPos == −1) {
      return false
   }

Now the script checks that there is a period after the @ sign. If not, you get a false result.

9. if (periodPos+3 > email.length) {
      return false
      }
   return true
   }

Finally, the script requires that there be at least two characters after the period in the address. If you made it this far without a false result, then the value of the function validEmail is true, meaning you have a good email address.

10. Now that you know whether or not the address is any good, you need to tell the script what to do with this newfound knowledge.

function submitIt(form) {
   if (!validEmail(form.emailAddr.value)) {
      alert("Invalid email address")
      form.emailAddr.focus()
      form.emailAddr.select()
      return false
   }
   return true
}

After defining the function submitIt, the if statement says that if the validEmail variable is not true, then put up an alert message saying "Invalid email address." When the user clicks the OK button on the alert box, the script returns the cursor to the form's email field, called emailAddr with the focus() command. Then it selects the contents of the emailAddr field with the select() command.

Figure 5.3 Pop-up menus are good to use when you have more choices than can comfortably fit in a group of radio buttons.

Script 5.2 Requiring the user to pick from a pop-up menu is easy.

```
script
<SCRIPT LANGUAGE="JavaScript">
<!-- Hide script from older browsers
function submitIt(form) {
  colorChoice = form.color.selectedIndex
  if (form.color.options[colorChoice].
  →value == "") {
    alert("You must pick a color")
    return false
  }
  return true
}
// End hiding script -->
</SCRIPT>
```

Selecting menu items

In the Car Picker example, prospective car buyers are given a choice of a whopping three colors: Red, Green, or Blue, as shown in Figure 5.3. When the menu is not pulled down, the user sees the helpful message "Choose a color." Because a car must have a color, you'll want to verify that the user actually picked one of the colors and didn't skip this item. The short Script 5.2 is all it takes.

To require a menu choice:

1. function submitIt(form) {

   This defines the submitIt function, which operates on the contents of the form.

2. colorChoice = form.color.selectedIndex

   The colorChoice variable gets a numerical result based on the color the user picked. No choice would be zero; Red, 1; Green, 2; and Blue, 3. The number refers to the order of the choice in the menu.

3. if (form.color.options[colorChoice].
   → value == " ") {
       alert("You must pick a color")
       return false

   Now we check the value of colorChoice. If the value is zero (== ""), then the form prompts the user with a message.

4. }
       return true
   }

   Otherwise, things are fine, and it's time to move on to the next validation task.

Working with radio buttons

Radio buttons are an either-or interface element that let the user pick one (and only one) choice within a group of options. Radio buttons should be used when one of those options is required. As shown in Figure 5.4, the form uses radio buttons to let the hypothetical car buyer choose between a two-door or four-door automobile. In this case, you can only pick one of these choices, and you must make a choice. If you don't, the form makes one for you, called the default choice.

As seen in Script 5.3, it doesn't take much to check that one button gets clicked. We use the same technique we did earlier in this chapter, where we loop through each button and check its status, then put up an error message if no button is picked.

Figure 5.4 Radio buttons are the best way to let the user pick only one choice from a group of options.

Script 5.3 Only one radio button may be checked, and this JavaScript is there to enforce the interface law.

```
<SCRIPT LANGUAGE="JavaScript">
 <!-- Hide script from older browsers
 function submitIt(form) {
   doorOption = -1
   for (i=0; i<form.DoorCt.length; i++) {
     if (form.DoorCt[i].checked)
       doorOption = i
   }
   if (doorOption == -1) {
     alert("You must choose 2 or 4 door")
     return false
   }
   return true
 }
 // End hiding script -->
</SCRIPT>
```

To make sure that the user picks a radio button:

1. function submitIt(form) {
    doorOption = -1

Define the function submitIt, and set the variable doorOption to -1, which is obviously not a valid number of car doors.

2.   for (i=0; i<form.DoorCt.length; i++) {

Now start the loop. The i counter gets set to zero, and as long as i is less than the number of radio buttons on the form, we add 1 to i with the i++ operator.

3. if (form.DoorCt[i].checked)
    doorOption = i
}

This is the test within the loop: if the radio button is checked, then doorOption is set to the value of i.

4. if (doorOption == -1) {
    alert("You must choose 2 or 4 door")
    return false
}

If you get to this point and the value of doorOption is still -1, then the form displays an alert dialog that tells the user that a choice must be made.

5. return true
}

If doorOption is reset, then something must have been picked. The script returns a true result, and you're out of the script.

WORKING WITH RADIO BUTTONS

Setting one field with another

With your forms, you'll often find that if the user makes one choice, that choice will dictate the value of other fields on the form. For example, let's say that the sunroof option is only available on a two-door model. You could deal with this in two ways. First, you could check the entry and put up an alert dialog if the user makes the wrong choice, as in Script 5.4. But it's a slicker design to simply make the entry for the user. So if they pick the sunroof, the script automatically clicks the two-door button. Script 5.5 shows you how.

As in the radio button section, you first have to make sure that the user clicked a door option. Note that the first part of the code in Script 5.4 is the same as in the previous section.

To check for proper entry:

1. if (form.DoorCt[doorOption].value ==
→ "fourDoor" && form.sunroof.checked) {
   alert("The sunroof is only available on the
   → two door model")
   return false
}
return true
}

This is pretty straightforward. If the value of the radio button is "fourDoor," and the sunroof check box is checked, then put up the error alert box. Otherwise, you're done.

Script 5.4 A simple way to notify a user is to alert the user when they make a mistake in data entry.

```
<SCRIPT LANGUAGE="JavaScript">
 <!-- Hide script from older browsers
 function submitIt(form) {
   // make sure they enter in a number of doors
   doorOption = -1
   for (i=0; i<form.DoorCt.length; i++) {
     if (form.DoorCt[i].checked)
       doorOption = i
   }
   // can't have the sunroof with a four door
   if (form.DoorCt[doorOption].value ==
→ "fourDoor" && form.sunroof.checked) {
     alert("The sunroof is only available on the
     → two door model")
     return false
   }
   // If we made it to here, everything's valid,
   → so return true
   return true
 }
 // End hiding script -->
</SCRIPT>
```

Script 5.5 A more sophisticated option lets you control field entries based on other choices made by the user.

```
script
<SCRIPT LANGUAGE="JavaScript">
<!-- Hide script from older browsers
function doorSet(sunroofField) {
  // If they picked the sunroof, force the two
  →door model
  if (sunroofField.checked) {
    for (i=0; i<document.carForm.DoorCt.length;
    →i++) {
      if (document.carForm.DoorCt[i].value ==
      →"twoDoor") {
        document.carForm.DoorCt[i].checked =
        →true
      }
    }
  }
}
// End hiding script -->
</SCRIPT>
```

To set a field value automatically:

Now take a look at Script 5.5.

1. function doorSet(sunroofField) {

   As usual, first you'll define the function.

2. if (sunroofField.checked) {
       for (i=0; i<document.carForm.DoorCt.
   → length; i++) {

   Next, if the sunroof box is checked, start up a loop where you scan through all of the doorCt fields.

3. if (document.carForm.DoorCt[i].value == "twoDoor") {

   You're looking for the two-door field.

4. document.carForm.DoorCt[i].checked = true

   Once you find the two-door field, select it by setting its value to true.

SETTING ONE FIELD WITH ANOTHER

Validating Zip codes

Those wacky users can type almost anything into a form, so you'll want to make sure that Zip code fields contain only numbers. Script 5.6 shows you how.

To make sure Zip codes are numeric:

1. function isNum(passedVal) {

First, define the function isNum. The variable passedVal was sent to the JavaScript from the form.

2. if (passedVal == "") {

    return false

}

If passedVal is empty, then the Zip code isn't numeric, and the function is false, and the script should put up an error message.

3. for (i=0; i<passedVal.length; i++) {

Now scan through the length of passedVal, incrementing the i counter each time it goes through the loop.

4. if (passedVal.charAt(i) < "0") {

    return false

}

if (passedVal.charAt(i) > "9") {

    return false

}

The charAt operator checks the character at the position i. If the character is less than "0" or greater than "9," it isn't a digit, so bail out and declare the input to be non-numeric, or false. If the result is true, you've got a numeric Zip code.

Script 5.6 Banish incorrect letters from your Zip codes with just a few lines of JavaScript.

```
<SCRIPT LANGUAGE="JavaScript">
<!-- Hide script from older browsers
function isNum(passedVal) {
// Is this a number?
  if (passedVal == "") {
    return false
  }
  for (i=0; i<passedVal.length; i++) {
    if (passedVal.charAt(i) < "0") {
      return false
    }
    if (passedVal.charAt(i) > "9") {
      return false
    }
  }
  return true
}
function validZip(inZip) {
// Is this a valid Zip code?
  if (inZip == "") {
    return true
  }
  if (isNum(inZip)) {
  // Check if Zip is numeric
    return true
  }
  return false
}
function submitIt(form) {
  if (!validZip(form.zip.value)) {
    alert("That is an invalid Zip code")
    form.zip.focus()
    form.zip.select()
    return false
  }
  return true
}
// End hiding script -->
</SCRIPT>
```

VALIDATING ZIP CODES

Figure 5.5 Make sure that passwords are entered correctly.

Script 5.7 Use scripts to compare the value of one field to another. Do they match?

```
<SCRIPT LANGUAGE="JavaScript">
  function validForm (form) {
    if (form.passwd1.value == "") {
      alert("You must enter a password")
      form.passwd1.focus()
      return false
    }
    if (form.passwd1.value != form.passwd2.value) {
      alert("Entered passwords did not match")
      form.passwd1.focus()
      form.passwd1.select()
      return false
    }
    return true
  }
</SCRIPT>
```

Figure 5.6 An alert box lets the user know that they made a mistake.

Verifying passwords

Whenever you're asking the user to enter a password that will be required in the future, you'll want to make the user type it in twice, to be sure that they didn't type it incorrectly, as shown in Figure 5.5. If both instances of the password don't match, then the script (Script 5.7) lets the user know with a helpful alert box, as in Figure 5.6.

To verify a password entry:

1. function validForm (form) {
    if (form.passwd1.value == " ") {
        alert("You must enter a password")
        form.passwd1.focus()

After defining the function, check to see if the value of the **passwd1** field is empty, as shown by the expression == " ". If so, put up an alert box that demands an entry and return the cursor to the **passwd1** field.

2. if (form.passwd1.value ! =
→ form.passwd2.value) {
    alert("Entered passwords did not match")
    form.passwd1.focus()
    form.passwd1.select()
    return false
}

If the value in **passwd1** is not equal to the value in **passwd2**, then it's time for another alert box. This time you return them to the **passwd1** field and select its contents, ready for the presumably bad contents to be replaced.

Script 5.8 Here's the entire HTML page, including all of the JavaScript, for the "Car Picker" example.

A COMPLETE FORM SCRIPT

```
                              Car Picker
<HTML>
<HEAD>
 <TITLE>Car Picker</TITLE>
 <SCRIPT LANGUAGE=JAVASCRIPT>
  <!-- Hide script from older browsers
```

```
 function validEmail(email) {                                                  Script 5.1
   invalidChars = " /:,;"

   if (email == "") {                        // cannot be empty
    return false
   }
   for (i=0; i<invalidChars.length; i++) {   // does it contain any invalid characters?
    badChar = invalidChars.charAt(i)
    if (email.indexOf(badChar,0) > -1) {
      return false
    }
   }
   atPos = email.indexOf("@",1)              // there must be one "@" symbol
   if (atPos == -1) {
    return false
   }
   if (email.indexOf("@",atPos+1) != -1) {  // and only one "@" symbol
    return false
   }
   periodPos = email.indexOf(".",atPos)
   if (periodPos == -1) {                    // and at least one "." after the "@"
    return false
   }
   if (periodPos+3 > email.length) {         // must be at least 2 characters after the "."
    return false
   }
   return true
 }
```

```
 function isNum(passedVal) {                 // Is this a number?                Script 5.6
   if (passedVal == "") {
    return false
   }
   for (i=0; i<passedVal.length; i++) {
    if (passedVal.charAt(i) < "0") {
      return false
    }
    if (passedVal.charAt(i) > "9") {
      return false
    }
   }
   return true
 }

 function validZip(inZip) {                  // Is this a valid Zip code?
   if (inZip == "") {
    return true
   }
   if (isNum(inZip)) {                       // Check if Zip is numeric
    return true
   }
   return false
 }
```

Script 5.8 (continued)

```
                              Car Picker
```

```
  function submitIt(form) {                      // make sure they enter a color
    colorChoice = form.color.selectedIndex                              Script 5.2
    if (form.color.options[colorChoice].value == "") {
      alert("You must pick a color")
      return false
    }

    // make sure they enter in a number of doors                       Script 5.3
    doorOption = -1
    for (i=0; i<form.DoorCt.length; i++) {
      if (form.DoorCt[i].checked)
        doorOption = i
    }
    if (doorOption == -1) {
      alert("You must choose 2 or 4 door")
      return false
    }

    // can't have the sunroof with a four door                         Script 5.4
    if (form.DoorCt[doorOption].value == "fourDoor" && form.sunroof.checked) {
      alert("The sunroof is only available on the two door model")
      return false
    }

    // check to see if the email's valid                               Script 5.1
    if (!validEmail(form.emailAddr.value)) {
      alert("Invalid email address")
      form.emailAddr.focus()
      form.emailAddr.select()
      return false
    }

    if (form.zip.value == "" && form.dealerList.selectedIndex == -1) {
      alert("You must either enter a Zip code, or pick the dealer closest to you")
      form.zip.focus()
      return false
    }

    if (!validZip(form.zip.value)) {                                   Script 5.6
      alert("That is an invalid Zip code")
      form.zip.focus()
      form.zip.select()
      return false
    }

    // If we made it to here, everything's valid, so return true
    return true
  }

  function doorSet(sunroofField) {                                     Script 5.5
    if (sunroofField.checked) {
      for (i=0; i<document.myForm.DoorCt.length; i++) {
        if (document.myForm.DoorCt[i].value == "twoDoor") {
          document.myForm.DoorCt[i].checked = true
        }
      }
    }
  }
// End hiding script -->
</SCRIPT>
</HEAD>
```

(This script continues on the next page.)

Script 5.8 *(continued)*

```
                                          Car Picker

<BODY BGCOLOR=WHITE>

<CENTER><FONT SIZE=+3>Car Picker</FONT></CENTER>

<FORM onSubmit="return submitIt(this)" ACTION="someAction.cgi" NAME=myForm>
<TABLE BORDER=0 CELLSPACING=8 CELLPADDING=8>
<TR>
<TD COLSPAN=5>
 Your Email Address: <INPUT NAME="emailAddr" TYPE="text" SIZE=30>
</TD></TR>
<TR>
<TD>Colors:</TD>
<TD COLSPAN=4>
 <SELECT NAME="color">
    <OPTION VALUE="" SELECTED>Choose a color
    <OPTION VALUE="red">Red
    <OPTION VALUE="green">Green
    <OPTION VALUE="blue">Blue
 </SELECT>
</TD></TR>
<TR>
<TD>Options:</TD>
<TD NOWRAP>
 <INPUT TYPE="checkbox" NAME="sunroof" VALUE="yes" onClick="doorSet(this)">Sunroof (Two door only)
</TD>
<TD NOWRAP>
 <INPUT TYPE="checkbox" NAME="pSteering" VALUE="yes">Power Steering
</TD>
<TD>
 <INPUT TYPE="checkbox" NAME="pBrakes" VALUE="yes">Power Brakes
</TD>
<TD>
 <INPUT TYPE="checkbox" NAME="fMats" VALUE="yes">Floor Mats
</TD></TR>
<TR>
<TD NOWRAP>Doors:</TD>
<TD COLSPAN=4>
 <INPUT TYPE="radio" VALUE="twoDoor" NAME="DoorCt">Two
 <INPUT TYPE="radio" VALUE="fourDoor" NAME="DoorCt">Four
</TD></TR>
<TR><TD COLSPAN=5>
Either enter your Zip code, or pick the dealer nearest you:

<P>Zip: <INPUT NAME="zip" TYPE="text" SIZE=5 MAXLENGTH=5>  
<SELECT NAME="dealerList" SIZE=4>
 <OPTION>California--Lemon Grove
 <OPTION>California--Lomita
 <OPTION>California--Long Beach
 <OPTION>California--Los Alamitos
 <OPTION>California--Los Angeles
</SELECT></P>

<P><INPUT TYPE="submit" VALUE="Submit">
<INPUT TYPE="reset" VALUE="Reset"></TD></TR></TABLE>
</FORM>
</BODY>
</HTML>
```

WORKING WITH BROWSER WINDOWS

The window is the most important interface element in a Web browser, and as you might expect, JavaScript provides you with many tools to manipulate windows.

In this chapter, you'll learn how to use JavaScript to open new windows, create windows that you can use as control panels, and write information into a window under script control.

Opening a new window

You'll often want to create new windows, to show users additional information without losing the information that they are reading. For example, you could open up an annotations window for a technical paper, or for a news story. Although it is possible to open a new browser window with HTML, using JavaScript gives you more control over the new window's content and features. Figure 6.1 shows you a standard browser window with all the parts labeled. You can create windows that have any or all of these parts. Script 6.1 shows you how to create a window from a page (Figure 6.2) where clicking on a link brings up a new window (that contains a map, in this example).

Script 6.1 Use this script to open a new window.

```
<HTML>
<HEAD>

<TITLE>Window Test</TITLE>
<SCRIPT LANGUAGE=JAVASCRIPT>
 <!-- Hide script from old browsers

 function newWindow() {
   mapWindow = window.open('barnum.gif',
   →'mapWin', 'width=500,height=400')
 }

 // End hiding script from old browsers -->
</SCRIPT>

</HEAD>
<BODY BGCOLOR=WHITE>
<CENTER><H1>Los Angeles Macintosh Group General
→Meeting</H1>
<H3>Featuring (again) the fabulous Tom and Dori
→show</H3>

<A HREF="javascript:newWindow()">Click here</A>
→for a map
</CENTER></BODY>
</HTML>
```

Figure 6.1 The elements of a browser window. The names in this figure correspond to the parameters you can apply in the open( ) command.

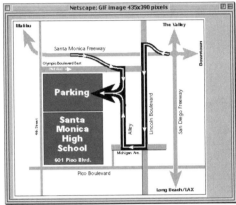

Figure 6.2 Opening a new window.

Adding parameters to windows

To add one or more of the parameters listed in Figure 6.1 to your windows, state them in the open() command enclosed in single quotes, with =yes after the name of a feature you want and =no after one you don't want. For example, if you want a window of a specified size with a toolbar, location box, and scrollbars, you would type

'toolbar=yes,location=yes,scrollbars=yes,
→ width=300,height=300'

as part of the open() command. Note that the window created would not have directory buttons, a status bar, and would not be resizable.

To open a new window:

1. function newWindow() {

First, define a function called newWindow().

2. mapWindow = window.open('barnum.gif',
→ 'mapWin', 'width=500,height=400')
}

The variable mapWindow has an open window object, containing the image file barnum.gif. The name of this new window is mapWin. Names are required, because you might want to reference this window later in a link or in another script. The new window has a width of 500 pixels and a height of 400 pixels; these parameters are optional.

3. <A HREF="javascript:newWindow()">
→ Click here</A>

In the link tag, you tell JavaScript to run the newWindow function when the link is clicked.

Scrolling a window

When you open a new window, you may want to have the window scroll to feature important information that you wish the user to see. In Script 6.2, we open a map and scroll the window to the actual meeting location (Figure 6.3).

To scroll a window:

1. function newWindow() {

   Define the function newWindow.

2. mapWindow = window.open('barnum.gif',
   → 'mapWin', 'toolbar=yes,location=yes,
   → scrollbars=yes,width=300,height=300')

   Set the parameters of the new window, and store them in the variable mapWindow.

3. setTimeout('mapWindow.scroll(0,100)',1000)
   }

   This is where the scrolling occurs. You've set the mapWindow variable to scroll 0 pixels horizontally, and 100 pixels vertically. The scrolling command is enclosed in the **setTimeout** command because the window must be created before it can be scrolled. Therefore, we have to wait a second (1000 milliseconds) and let the window be generated.

Script 6.2 The script opens and scrolls through a new window.

```
<HTML>
<HEAD>

<TITLE>Window Scrolling Example</TITLE>
<SCRIPT LANGUAGE=JAVASCRIPT>
 <!-- Hide script from old browsers
 function newWindow() {
    mapWindow = window.open('barnum.gif',
    →'mapWin', 'toolbar=yes,location=yes,
    →scrollbars=yes,width=300,height=300')

    setTimeout('mapWindow.scroll(0,100)',1000)
 }

 // End hiding script from old browsers -->
</SCRIPT>

</HEAD>
<BODY BGCOLOR=WHITE>
<CENTER><H1>Los Angeles Macintosh Group General
→Meeting</H1>
<H3>Featuring (again) the fabulous Tom and Dori
→show</H3>

<A HREF="javascript:newWindow()">Click here</A>
→for a map
</CENTER></BODY>
</HTML>
```

Figure 6.3 When the user clicks the link, the new window opens and scrolls to the important information.

✔ Tips

- Unlike Netscape, Internet Explorer can't scroll a window if the window contains a URL from another server. You can only scroll content on your machine with Microsoft Internet Explorer.

- You can only scroll windows with Netscape Navigator 3.0 or higher, or Microsoft Internet Explorer 3.0 or higher.

SCROLLING A WINDOW

Bringing windows to the front

When you create more than one window, you often want to control which one shows up in front, so that the user knows which window to use. In this example, we'll load a page (Figure 6.4) which will use Script 6.3 to create two smaller windows. The page will have links that, when clicked, bring the smaller windows to the front.

To bring windows to the front:

1. mapWindow = window.open('barnum.gif',
→ 'mapWin', 'toolbar=yes,scrollbars=yes,
→ width=300,height=300')

As usual, start by creating a variable and filling it with the window.open command and its parameters. This is the window with the map in it (Figure 6.5).

2. directionsWindow =
→ window.open('window12a.html', 'pageWin',
→ 'width=225,height=200')

Repeat the process to create the directions window (Figure 6.6).

3. function mapToFront() {

Here we're defining the function mapToFront().

Figure 6.4 The main window; clicking on a link brings the appropriate window to the front.

Figure 6.5 The map window, when it is called to the front.

Figure 6.6 The directions window, when it is called to the front.

Script 6.3 This script brings either of the two smaller windows to the front. The second page is just the HTML for the directions window.

```
script

<HTML>
<HEAD>

<TITLE>Front Window</TITLE>
<SCRIPT LANGUAGE=JAVASCRIPT>
 <!-- Hide script from old browsers
 mapWindow = window.open('barnum.gif', 'mapWin',
 →'toolbar=yes,scrollbars=yes,width=300,
 →height=300')

 directionsWindow = window.open('window12a.html',
 →'pageWin', 'width=225,height=200')

 function mapToFront() {
   mapWindow.focus()
 }

 function directionsToFront() {
   directionsWindow.focus()
 }

 // End hiding script from old browsers -->
</SCRIPT>

</HEAD>
<BODY BGCOLOR=WHITE>
<CENTER><H1>LAMG General Meeting</H1>
<H3>Featuring (again) the fabulous Tom and Dori
→show</H3>

<A HREF="javascript:mapToFront()">Look at the
→map</a>  
<A HREF="javascript:directionsToFront()">Look at
→the directions</a>

</CENTER></BODY>
</HTML>
```

```
script

<HTML>
<HEAD>

<TITLE>Directions</TITLE>

</HEAD>
<BODY BGCOLOR=WHITE>
<H1>How to get there</H1>
Blah, blah, blah, blah, blah, blah, blah, blah,
→blah, blah, blah, blah, blah, blah, blah, blah,
→blah, blah, blah, blah, blah, blah, blah, blah,
→blah, blah, blah, blah, blah, blah, blah, blah,
→blah, blah, blah, blah, blah, blah, blah, blah,
→blah, blah, blah, blah, blah, blah, blah, blah,
→blah, blah
</BODY>
</HTML>
```

4. mapWindow.focus()
   }

This line of code makes mapWindow the focus, which means that the script pulls the mapWindow window to the front of the layers of windows.

5. function directionsToFront() {
   directionsWindow.focus()
   }

This code creates the directionsToFront() function, which when called makes the directionsWindow window the focus.

6. <A HREF="javascript:mapToFront()">
   → Look at the map</a>

Clicking on this link tells JavaScript to run the mapToFront function, which brings the map window to the top.

7. <A HREF="javascript:directionsToFront()">
   → Look at the directions</a>

And clicking on this link tells JavaScript to run the directionsToFront function, which will bring the directions window to the top.

✔ Tip

- The opposite of the focus() command in Steps 4 and 5 is the blur() command. Where focus() brings a target window to the top of the layers of windows, blur() pushes the target to the back of the windows.

Updating one window from another

If you deal with forms and data entered by your users, you'll want to know how to send information entered in one window to another window for display. You might use this in a situation where you are selling a product to replicate the user's information in a summary window. In this example, we'll use two windows: the main window is the parent window, which will receive and display information entered in a child window. Script 6.4 shows the script for the parent window.

To update one window from another:

1. newWindow =
   → window.open('window11a.html', 'newWin',
   → 'toolbar=yes,location=yes,scrollbars=yes,
   → width=300,height=100')

   This line of script in the parent window tells the browser to create the child window, using the window11a.html file. The rest of the line specifies the child window's parameters (Figure 6.8).

2. <FORM NAME=outputForm>

   There is a rudimentary form on the parent page (Figure 6.7), designed so that the script can easily fill in a text field with the information it will be getting from the child window. This line opens the FORM tag and gives the form a name.

Script 6.4 The parent window script.

```
<HTML>
<HEAD>

<TITLE>Big Window</TITLE>
</HEAD>
<BODY BGCOLOR=WHITE>
<SCRIPT LANGUAGE=JAVASCRIPT>
 <!-- Hide script from old browsers

 newWindow = window.open('window11a.html',
 →'newWin', 'toolbar=yes,location=yes,
 →scrollbars=yes,width=300,height=100')

 // End hiding script from old browsers -->
</SCRIPT>

<CENTER><H1>Welcome to this page!</H1>
<FORM NAME=outputForm>
<INPUT TYPE=TEXT SIZE=20 NAME=msgLine VALUE="">
</FORM></CENTER></BODY>
</HTML>
```

Figure 6.7 The initial parent window.

Figure 6.8 The child window is where the user enters data.

Script 6.5 The child window script.

```
script

<HTML>
<HEAD>

<TITLE>Little Window</TITLE>
<SCRIPT LANGUAGE=JAVASCRIPT>
 <!-- Hide script from old browsers

 function updateParent(textField) {
   opener.document.outputForm.msgLine.value =
   →"Hello " + textField.value + "!"
 }

 // End hiding script from old browsers -->
</SCRIPT>

</HEAD>
<BODY BGCOLOR=WHITE>
<H1>What's your name?</H1>
<FORM>
<INPUT TYPE=TEXT ONBLUR=
→"javascript:updateParent(this)" SIZE=20>
</FORM>

</BODY>
</HTML>
```

Figure 6.9 The updated parent window after calling information from the child window.

3. <INPUT TYPE=TEXT SIZE=20
→ NAME=msgLine VALUE=""></FORM>

This line specifies that the form will contain text with a maximum length of 20 characters, and names the text field msgLine. It also initializes the field with a null value, that is, starts out the field empty, and closes the FORM tag.

Now turn to the script from the child window (see Script 6.5).

4. function updateParent(textField) {

Here you create the updateParent function. The textField variable is the contents of the form in the child page.

5. opener.document.outputForm.msgLine.value
→ = "Hello " + textField.value + "!"

This line introduces the opener property, which is how JavaScript references back to the parent document that opened the child window. This line tells the opener document window to look at the form outputForm, find the field called msg.Line, and insert the value of the expression after the equals sign. That expression takes the word "Hello," adds on the value of textField, then appends an exclamation point.

6. <FORM>
<INPUT TYPE=TEXT ONBLUR=
→ "javascript:updateParent(this)"
→ SIZE=20></FORM>

This is the FORM tag in the child HTML page. It sets up the text field, and says to run the updateParent function onBlur, that is, when the user leaves the text field after entering data. The result in the parent window is seen in Figure 6.9.

Creating new pages with JavaScript

Previous multiple-window examples in this chapter used more than one HTML file to create the different windows. But there's no need to do that, since you can embed HTML within a script and create a new HTML page on the fly. This is especially useful because you can use the power of JavaScript to fill the new page with dynamic content. Script 6.6 is a fairly simple example; in this page (Figure 6.10), you'll create a new HTML page, then increment a loop that adds 100 lines of text to the page.

To create a new page with JavaScript:

1. newWindow = window.open('', 'newWin',
   → 'toolbar=yes,location=yes,scrollbars=yes,
   → resizable=yes,width=300,height=300')

   This line opens the new window, sets its parameters, and assigns it to the variable newWindow.

2. newWindow.document.write
   → ("<HTML><HEAD><TITLE>
   → Generated Window</TITLE></HEAD>
   → <BODY BGCOLOR=WHITE><H2>
   → This window shows the result from the
   → other window</H2>")

   This is the cool part. Here, the script is writing into the document window represented by newWindow. You're generating the HTML headers and the first part of the page body (see Figure 6.11).

Script 6.6 You can create new HTML pages entirely under scripted control.

```
<HTML>
<HEAD>

<TITLE>Main Window</TITLE>
</HEAD>
<BODY BGCOLOR=WHITE>
<CENTER><H1>This window is looping madly!</H1>

<SCRIPT LANGUAGE=JAVASCRIPT>
 <!-- Hide script from old browsers
 newWindow = window.open('', 'newWin',
 → 'toolbar=yes,location=yes,scrollbars=yes,
 →resizable=yes,width=300,height=300')
 newWindow.document.write
 →("<HTML><HEAD><TITLE>Generated Window</TITLE>
 →</HEAD><BODY BGCOLOR=WHITE><H2>This window
 →shows the result from the other window</H2>")

 for (i=0; i<100; i++) {
   newWindow.document.writeln("<BR>The loop is
   →now at: " + i)
 }
 newWindow.document.write("</BODY></HTML>")
 newWindow.document.close()

 // End hiding script from old browsers -->
</SCRIPT>
</BODY>
</HTML>
```

Figure 6.10 This parent window is writing into the child window ...

Figure 6.11 ... and the child window shows the result.

3. for (i=0; i<100; i++) {

You're starting a loop with the counter variable i. Set i to zero to begin, then as long as i is less than 100, you increment the value of i by 1.

4. newWindow.document.writeln("
→ The loop is now at: " + i)
}

Within the loop, the code writes text to the page using the document.write command. In this line, the script writes to the newWindow document window. The writeln command automatically adds a return character after each text string it writes to the document, but you still have to add a <BR> to insert a line break. The string includes the value of i, which is updated every time through the loop.

5. newWindow.document.write
→ ("</BODY></HTML>")

Here's where you write the closing part of the HTML page code.

6. newWindow.document.close()

Finally, you need to tell the browser that you're done writing to the newWindow document with the close() command.

Closing a window

Just as you can create windows, you should know how to destroy windows by closing them. In Script 6.7, the parent window has open and close links that create and destroy the child window.

To close a window:

1. function openWindow() {
newWindow = window.open
→ ('', 'newWin', 'toolbar=yes,location=yes,
→ scrollbars=yes,width=300,height=200')
}

This is the now-familiar function definition, with the newWindow object being assigned with the window parameters.

2. function closeWindow() {
    newWindow.close()
}

The new function closeWindow() applies the command close to the newWindow object.

3. <A HREF="javascript:openWindow()">
→ Open a new window</A>

Clicking the "Open a new window" link in Figure 6.12 calls the openWindow function and creates a new window.

4. <A HREF="javascript:closeWindow()">
→ Close the window</A>

5. Similarly, clicking the "Close the window" link in Figure 6.12 calls the closeWindow function and destroys the child window.

Script 6.7 This script opens and closes a child window.

```
<HTML>
<HEAD>

<TITLE>Window Test</TITLE>
<SCRIPT LANGUAGE=JAVASCRIPT>
 <!-- Hide script from old browsers
 function openWindow() {
   newWindow = window.open('', 'newWin',
   →'toolbar=yes,location=yes,scrollbars=yes,
   →width=300,height=200')
 }

 function closeWindow() {
   newWindow.close()
 }

 // End hiding script from old browsers -->
</SCRIPT>

</HEAD>
<BODY BGCOLOR=WHITE>
<CENTER><H1>Let's play with windows!</H1>

<H3><A HREF="javascript:openWindow()">
→Open a new window</A>  
→<A HREF="javascript:closeWindow()">
→Close the window</A></H3>
</CENTER></BODY>
</HTML>
```

Figure 6.12 The links in this window create and destroy a child window. Note the openWindow function about to be called, as shown in the status bar.

Script 6.8 This script sets up the control panel.

```
                    script
<HTML>
<HEAD>

<TITLE>Parent Window</TITLE>
<SCRIPT LANGUAGE=JAVASCRIPT>
 <!-- Hide script from old browsers

 newWindow = window.open('panel.html',
 →'newWin', 'width=225,height=200')

 // End hiding script from old browsers -->
</SCRIPT>

</HEAD>
<BODY BGCOLOR=WHITE>
<CENTER><H1>JavaScript for the World Wide Web,
→2nd Edition</H1>
<H2>by Tom Negrino and Dori Smith</H2>
<IMG SRC="javascript2ed.gif" WIDTH="109"
→HEIGHT="140" BORDER="0">
</CENTER></BODY>
</HTML>
```

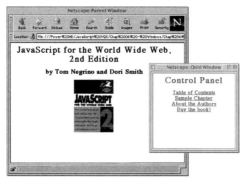

Figure 6.13 The parent window and the child control panel window.

Creating a control panel

Using a child window as a control panel, that is, one window that contains controls that affect other windows, opens a world of possibilities in Web site interface design. You can use control panels to assist the ways in which users interact with your site, and control panels are also useful for applications such as informational kiosks.

To create a control panel:

1. newWindow = window.open('panel.html',
    → 'newWin', 'width=225,height=200')

    The only thing the script in Script 6.8 does is open up a new window (the control panel), using the HTML in the file panel.html. You get two windows, as shown in Figure 6.13. Now turn to Script 6.9.

    (Continued)

2. function updateParent(newURL) {

Now you're working in panel.html; the code is shown in Script 6.9. This line defines the new function updateParent as containing the value of the variable newURL.

3. opener.document.location = newURL
}

This line tells the opener (the parent document) to take its location property (the HTML page it is displaying) from the variable newURL.

4. <A HREF=
→ "javascript:updateParent('toc.html')">
→ Table of Contents</A>

Clicking on the "Table of Contents" link triggers the updateParent function, and fills newURL with the name of the HTML page toc.html. The parent page obediently loads that page, as seen in Figure 6.14. The rest of the links in the control panel work in the same fashion.

CREATING A CONTROL PANEL

Script 6.9 The control panel script determines which page will be displayed in the parent window.

```
script
<HTML>
<HEAD>

<TITLE>Child Window</TITLE>
<SCRIPT LANGUAGE=JAVASCRIPT>
 <!-- Hide script from old browsers

 function updateParent(newURL) {
   opener.document.location = newURL
 }

 // End hiding script from old browsers -->
</SCRIPT>

</HEAD>
<BODY BGCOLOR=WHITE>
<CENTER><H1>Control Panel</H1>
<H3><A HREF="javascript:updateParent
→('toc.html')">Table of Contents</A><BR>
<A HREF="javascript:updateParent
→('chapter.html')">Sample Chapter</A><BR>
<A HREF="javascript:updateParent
→('authors.html')">About the Authors</A><BR>
<A HREF="javascript:updateParent
→('buy.html')">Buy the book!</A></H3>
</CENTER></BODY>
</HTML>
```

Figure 6.14 Clicking the control panel loads the Table of Contents in the parent window.

Script 6.10 This extremely simple script puts up a modal alert box when the page loads.

```
<HTML>
<HEAD>

<TITLE>Window Test</TITLE>

</HEAD>
<BODY BGCOLOR=WHITE onload="alert('Welcome to
→this page!')">
<CENTER><H1>JavaScript for the World Wide Web,
→2E</H1>

</CENTER></BODY>
</HTML>
```

Figure 6.15 The resulting alert box.

Displaying alerts when a window is loaded

Occasionally, you might want to flash users a message when they load or reload a page. You can use an alert box to do the job. Script 6.10 shows how to create this very simple trick, and Figure 6.15 shows the result.

To display an alert when a window is loaded:

1. `<BODY BGCOLOR=WHITE onload=`
   → `"alert('Welcome to this page!')">`

   As part of the BODY tag, type onload="alert('message')" where message is whatever you want to put in the alert box.

✔ Tips

- Alert boxes are modal, that is, they wait for a user action. So, if the user is away from their computer, all processing on that computer may stop while the alert box is waiting for input. They can also annoy the user because they interrupt the user's work.

- Alert boxes may be more useful to you than to the user. That's because they can display just about anything, including JavaScript objects. This makes alert boxes valuable JavaScript debugging tools, because you can use them to display intermediate results from a calculation or the current value of a variable. See Chapter 11 for more about debugging.

- There's no way to get rid of the line of text in the alert box that indicates that the alert was generated by JavaScript (in Figure 6.15, this text is in the title bar; in older browsers, it can be elsewhere in the alert box). It's a security precaution to make sure that evil scripters don't make imitation alert boxes that could fool unsuspecting users into entering passwords or other sensitive information.

DYNAMICALLY UPDATED PAGES

Effective Web pages are a result of many different factors, including compelling content, good design, and attention to details, such as how fast the page loads. One of the ways to speed up page loads while still providing the user with an interesting and interactive experience is to use JavaScript to make individual page elements update within the user's browser. In other words, instead of your Web server pushing the page experience to the user, the server pushes the script over the phone lines. The script then uses the power of the user's computer to make the page come alive.

By moving the processing from the server side to the client (user) side, you get better performance and you can personalize the user experience to some extent.

In this chapter, you'll learn how to use JavaScript to display the local date and time on your Web pages; customize a greeting by the time of day where your user is; and send your users to different pages depending on what domain they're from, or what page they last visited.

Putting the current date into a Web page

JavaScript can determine the current date and time from your computer (which it gets as a number), and then manipulate that figure in many ways. Your script has to handle the conversion from a number into a textual date, however. Script 7.1 shows how to get the current date, convert it from a number into a standard date, and then write the result to a document window. Note that Script 7.1 actually contains two scripts, one in the head of the HTML document (the header script), and the other in the body of the document (unsurprisingly, we call it the body script).

To put the current date into a Web page:

1. var dayName = new Array
→ ("Sunday","Monday","Tuesday",
→ "Wednesday","Thursday","Friday",
→ "Saturday")

First, you need to create a new array that contains the days of the week. Make sure that you use commas to separate the items in the array, and because they are text strings, each item must be enclosed in quotes. The array gets assigned to the variable dayName.

2. var monName = new Array ("January",
→ "February", "March", "April", "May",
→ "June", "July", "August", "September",
→ "October", "November", "December")

In this step you're doing the same thing with month names, and assigning them to the brilliantly named monName variable.

3. var now = new Date

The last thing to do in this first script is to create a new date variable now with the new Date command, which tells JavaScript to create a new Date object, and fill it with the current date.

Script 7.1 This script is actually made up of two short scripts, and writes the current date to the document window.

```
script
<HTML>
<HEAD>

<TITLE>Dynamic Date Display</TITLE>

<SCRIPT LANGUAGE=JAVASCRIPT>
 <!-- Hide script from old browsers
 var dayName = new Array ("Sunday","Monday",
 →"Tuesday","Wednesday","Thursday","Friday",
 →"Saturday")
 var monName = new Array ("January", "February",
 →"March", "April", "May", "June", "July",
 →"August", "September", "October", "November",
 →"December")

 var now = new Date

 // End hiding script from old browsers -->
</SCRIPT>
</HEAD>
<BODY BGCOLOR=WHITE>

<SCRIPT LANGUAGE=JAVASCRIPT>
 <!-- Hide script from old browsers

 document.write("<H1>Today is " +
 →dayName[now.getDay()] + ", " +
 →monName[now.getMonth()] + " " +
 →now.getDate() + ".</H1>")

 // End hiding script from old browsers -->
</SCRIPT>

</BODY>
</HTML>
```

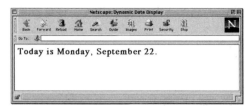

Figure 7.1 JavaScript dynamically displays the current date in the window.

JavaScript's inconsistent handling of time

As mentioned earlier in this book, JavaScript begins numbering at zero in most cases, so numbering begins with 0, 1, 2, 3, etc. But this isn't consistent with dates, which begin with the number 1. So if you have an array that deals with the days of the week, you'll have this:

Sunday = 0
Monday = 1
Tuesday = 2
Wednesday = 3
Thursday = 4
Friday = 5
Saturday = 6

In much the same way, the twelve months of the year are numbered from 0 through 11.

On the other hand, when you're dealing with the date of the month, it makes no sense to start at zero (personally, I've never heard of April 0), so JavaScript starts at 1.

Hours are dealt with from 0 (midnight) to 23 (11 PM), as with military time. Later in this chapter we'll show you how to convert from military time to AM/PM.

4. document.write("<H1>Today is " +
→ dayName[now.getDay()] + ", " +
→ monName[now.getMonth()] + " " +
→ now.getDate() + ".</H1>")

The second script area consists of just one line, and it writes directly to the document window (there's more about this technique in Chapter 6). The document.write command puts the expression within the parentheses into the document window.

The first element in the parentheses is a bit of HTML, the H1 tag, which makes the line you're writing a Heading 1 size, the largest heading size.

Follow that with the "Today is " text string (notice that there's a space after the second word), followed by the + sign which means concatenate (or add it on to) what follows.

The object dayName[now.getDay()] is read from right to left; getDay() is the JavaScript command that gets the day of the month, and adding now to it gets today's day of the week. The numerical result references one of the entries in the array dayName.

Next, you concatenate a comma to the text string that you're building, then concatenate the next expression, which is the month name, expressed by the object monName[now.getMonth()]. This gets the month in much the same fashion as getting the day name, and references one of the entries in the array monName.

A space is concatenated next, then comes the object now.getDate(), which gets the date of the month. We wrap up by concatenating a period to the text string, and closing the H1 tag. The result is shown in Figure 7.1.

Working with days

You might want to display a different message to your users if it's a weekend. Script 7.2 tells you how to do it.

To figure out if it is a weekend:

1. now = new Date

Fill the variable now with the current date.

2. if (now.getDay() > 0 && now.getDay() < 6) {

This extracts the numerical day of the week from the now variable and asks if it is greater than 0 (remember that Sunday is 0). Next the line uses the && operator, which is a logical and (i.e., both parts have to be true), and asks if now is less than 6, which is the number for Saturday.

3. document.write("Sorry, it's a weekday.")
}

If the result of the last expression is greater than 0 and less than 6, it has to be between 1 and 5, which is to say, from Monday to Friday, so the script writes out its sad message to the document window, as shown in Figure 7.2.

4. else {
    document.write("Hooray, it's a weekend!")
}

If we failed the test in the last step, it must be a weekend, and we write the happy news to the document window.

Script 7.2 This script figures out if it is a weekday or weekend.

```
<HTML>
<HEAD>
<TITLE>Weekend Checker</TITLE>
</HEAD>
<BODY BGCOLOR=WHITE>
<H1>
<SCRIPT LANGUAGE=JAVASCRIPT>
 <!-- Hide script from old browsers
 now = new Date

 if (now.getDay() > 0 && now.getDay() < 6) {
   document.write("Sorry, it's a weekday.")
 }
 else {
   document.write("Hooray, it's a weekend!")
 }

 // End hiding script from old browsers -->
</SCRIPT>
</H1>
</BODY>
</HTML>
```

Figure 7.2 The sad news gets written to the window.

Script 7.3 Scripts can be used to check what time of day it is, and react appropriately.

```
<HTML>
<HEAD>

<TITLE>What time is it? JavaScript
→knows...</TITLE>

</HEAD>
<BODY BGCOLOR=WHITE>
<H1>
<SCRIPT LANGUAGE=JAVASCRIPT>
 <!-- Hide script from old browsers
 now = new Date

 if (now.getHours() < 5) {
   document.write("What are you doing up so
   →late?")
 }
 else if (now.getHours() < 9) {
   document.write("Good Morning!")
 }
 else if (now.getHours() < 17) {
   document.write("No surfing during working
   →hours!")
 }
 else {
   document.write("Good Evening!")
 }

 // End hiding script from old browsers -->
</SCRIPT>
</H1>
</BODY>
</HTML>
```

Figure 7.3 It was definitely too late at night when we wrote this.

Customizing your message for the time of day

We can take the technique used in the last example and use it again to customize a message for the user, depending on the time of day. This is often used as a friendly greeting when a user enters a site. Script 7.3 shows how it is done, and Figure 7.3 shows how we were up writing way past our usual bedtime.

To customize messages for the time of day:

1. now = new Date
   if (now.getHours() < 5) {

   Once again, define the variable now and fill it with a new Date object. The getHours method extracts hours from the now variable, then tests to see if that number is less than 5 (which corresponds to 5 AM, since numbering in JavaScript starts at midnight).

2. document.write
   → ("What are you doing up so late?")
   }

   If it is before 5 AM, the script scolds the user by writing this message to the document window, as shown in Figure 7.3.

   The rest of the script repeats the above line, adjusting it for the time of day and writing out a different message. If it is between 6 AM and 9 AM, the script says "Good Morning!"; between 9 AM and 5 PM, it says "No surfing during working hours"; and after 5, it says "Good Evening!"

Converting military time to AM/PM

JavaScript provides the time in 24-hour format, also known as military time. Many people are unfamiliar or uncomfortable with this format, so you'll want to know how to convert it to 12-hour format. In Script 7.4, we see one way to go about the task, which needs a bit of explanation. The page we're creating uses a form containing a single text field into which we write the time, based on a function in the script. The form is controlled by two radio buttons, which let us switch the time from 24-hour format into 12-hour format. The result is shown in Figure 7.4.

To convert military time to AM/PM:

1. function showMilitaryTime() {
    if (document.theForm.showMilitary[0].
    → checked) {
      return true
    }
    return false
}

The first function in the script checks to see which radio button in the form the user has checked. The function showMilitaryTime says that if the document's form element showMilitary[0] is checked, then it should return a true result, otherwise it returns a false result.

2. function showTheHours(theHour) {

Next, we set up a function called showTheHours, containing the variable theHour.

(Continued)

Figure 7.4 The script in action.

Script 7.4 This script converts between 24-hour and 12-hour time.

```
                              script
<HTML>
<HEAD>
<TITLE>JavaScript Clock</TITLE>
<SCRIPT LANGUAGE=JAVASCRIPT>
 <!-- Hide script from old browsers
 function showMilitaryTime() {
   if (document.theForm.showMilitary[0].checked) {
     return true
   }
   return false
 }
 function showTheHours(theHour) {
   if (showMilitaryTime() || (theHour > 0 && theHour < 13)) {
     return (theHour)
   }
   if (theHour == 0) {
     return (12)
   }
   return (theHour-12)
 }
 function showZeroFilled(inValue) {
   if (inValue > 9) {
     return ":" + inValue
   }
   return ":0" + inValue
 }
 function showAmPm() {
   if (showMilitaryTime()) {
     return ("")
   }
   if (now.getHours() < 12) {
     return (" am")
   }
   return (" pm")
 }
 function showTheTime() {
   now = new Date
   document.theForm.showTime.value = showTheHours(now.getHours()) + showZeroFilled(now.getMinutes()) +
   ↪showZeroFilled(now.getSeconds()) + showAmPm()
   setTimeout("showTheTime()",1000)
 }
 // End hiding script from old browsers -->
</SCRIPT>
</HEAD>
<BODY BGCOLOR=WHITE ONLOAD="showTheTime()">
<CENTER><FORM name=theForm>
 <INPUT TYPE=TEXT NAME=showTime SIZE=11><P>
 Display Military Time?
 <INPUT TYPE=RADIO NAME=showMilitary CHECKED>Yes   
 <INPUT TYPE=RADIO NAME=showMilitary >No
</FORM></CENTER>
</BODY>
</HTML>
```

CONVERTING MILITARY TIME TO AM/PM

3. if (showMilitaryTime() ||
  → (theHour > 0 && theHour < 13)) {
     return (theHour)
  }

This line says that if the user wants to show military time, or if the result of the hour portion of the time is greater than zero but less than 13, then simply put that number into the variable theHour.

4. if (theHour == 0) {
     return (12)
     }
     return (theHour–12)
  }

If theHour is zero, then return with the result 12 (when the hour is 12 AM), otherwise return theHour minus 12 (which converts hours 13 and over to their civilian counterparts).

5. function showZeroFilled(inValue) {
     if (inValue > 9) {
        return ":" + inValue
     }
        return ":0" + inValue
  }

This function is used to pretty up the output; when the seconds figure is 9 or under, it pads the seconds figure with a leading zero.

6. function showAmPm() {
     if (showMilitaryTime()) {
        return ("")
     }

This function adds the AM or PM to the 12-hour time. If the function showMilitaryTime is true, it returns nothing, and goes to the next function.

7.
```
if (now.getHours() < 12) {
    return (" am")
}
    return (" pm")
}
```

If the hours portion of the now variable is less than 12, then the value of the function is AM, otherwise it is PM. Note that there is a leading space in the AM or PM text strings, so things look nice.

8.
```
function showTheTime() {
    now = new Date
```

Here's the meat (or for you vegetarians, the tofu) of the script. This function first fills the variable now with the current date.

9.
```
document.theForm.showTime.value =
→ showTheHours(now.getHours()) +
→ showZeroFilled(now.getMinutes()) +
→ showZeroFilled(now.getSeconds()) +
→ showAmPm()
```

This looks scary, but all it is doing is building the time value that goes into the form's field by concatenating the result from all of the other functions.

10.
```
setTimeout("showTheTime()",1000)
}
```

This final bit of code tells the display to update every second.

Creating a countdown

Sooner or later, you'll want to put a countdown on your pages that tells the user how many days or hours until a particular event. Script 7.5 lets one of the authors know his responsibilities, in no uncertain terms, as you can see in Figure 7.5. This is another technique that uses two scripts. The header script does all of the calculations, and the body script takes the calculation results, sticks them all together, and writes them out to the document window.

To create a countdown:

1. now = new Date

   Start by getting the date and sticking it into the now variable.

2. anniv = new Date (now.getYear(),6,21)
   if (anniv.getTime() < now.getTime()) {
       anniv.setYear(anniv.getYear()+1)
   }

   Here's the first of three similar functions. This one fills the anniv variable by getting the current year and then specifying the anniversary date, which is July 21. Sure, it says 6,21 above (not 7/21), but that's because month numbering begins with zero. So January is month 0 and July is month 6.

   Next we check if the anniversary time is less than the current time. If it is, we increment the year number by one. Repeat the process with minor changes for the birthday and xmas variables, which are set in the next two functions.

Script 7.5 How to make a countdown ...

```
<HTML>
<HEAD>

<TITLE>Dynamic Countdown</TITLE>

<SCRIPT LANGUAGE=JAVASCRIPT>
 <!-- Hide script from old browsers
 now = new Date

 anniv = new Date (now.getYear(),6,21)
 if (anniv.getTime() < now.getTime()) {
   anniv.setYear(anniv.getYear()+1)
 }

 birthday = new Date (now.getYear(),7,7)
 if (birthday.getTime() < now.getTime()) {
   birthday.setYear(birthday.getYear()+1)
 }

 xmas = new Date (now.getYear(),11,25)
 if (xmas.getTime() < now.getTime()) {
   xmas.setYear(xmas.getYear()+1)
 }

 function dayToDays(inTime) {
   return (Math.floor(inTime.getTime() /
   →(1000 * 60 * 60 * 24)))
 }

 function daysTill(inDate) {
   return dayToDays(inDate) - dayToDays(now)
 }

 // End hiding script from old browsers -->
</SCRIPT>

</HEAD>
<BODY BGCOLOR=WHITE>
<H1>Dori says:<BR><BR>

<SCRIPT LANGUAGE=JAVASCRIPT>
 <!-- Hide script from old browsers
 document.write("It's only " + daysTill(birthday)
 →+ " days until my birthday and " +
 →daysTill(xmas) + " days until Christmas--you'd
 →better start shopping now!")

 document.write("<p>And it's only "+
 →daysTill(anniv) +" days until our
 →anniversary...")

 // End hiding script from old browsers -->
</SCRIPT>
</H1>
</BODY>
</HTML>
```

Figure 7.5 ... and nag your loved one at the same time.

More weird time stuff

Month numbering in JavaScript begins with 0, day numbering with 1, and JavaScript can't deal with years prior to 1970.

The getTime method in JavaScript, for reasons probably best left unexplored, returns a number that is the number of milliseconds since January 1, 1970. Luckily, we hardly ever have to see that number, as there have been a whopping number of milliseconds in the past 27 or so years.

3. function dayToDays(inTime) {
　　return (Math.floor(inTime.getTime() /
　　→ (1000 * 60 * 60 * 24)))
}

JavaScript stores dates in milliseconds since January 1, 1970. In order to compare two dates, we change this to be the number of days since January 1, 1970. First, we get the number of milliseconds in a day by multiplying 1000 (the number of milliseconds in a second) by 60 (number of seconds in a minute), by 60 again (number of minutes in an hour), and then by 24 (number of hours in a day). Dividing the number of milliseconds returned by getTime() by this number gives the number of days since January 1, 1970. The Math.floor() function makes sure that our result is a whole number.

4. function daysTill(inDate) {
　　return dayToDays(inDate) –
　　→ dayToDays(now)
}

This function is passed a date inDate, and returns the number of days between inDate and the current date.

The code in the body script (beginning with document.write) is the now-familiar type that takes the results of calculations, then concatenates them together with text strings, and writes the whole mess to the document window.

CREATING A COUNTDOWN

Working with referrer pages

A referrer page is the page that the user was viewing before the current page, or in other words, the page the user came from. You may wish to provide a message to the user and mention the referrer page, as shown in Figure 7.6.

To display the referrer page:

1. if (document.referrer != "") {

   Script 7.6 is easy to understand. If the referrer page, represented here by document.referrer, is not empty then continue through the script. The document.referrer object could be empty if the user hadn't visited any other page before yours, i.e., if they opened their browser directly to your page.

2. document.write("<H1>I hope you like this
   → page better than " + document.referrer +
   → ".</H1>")
   }

   If the document.referrer object isn't empty, then write out a message to the document with a text string, concatenating the document.referrer into the middle of the string.

✔ Tip

■ This technique can also be harnessed to trigger different actions depending on what the referrer page was. You could find out the domain of the referrer page, and then serve up users who came from a particular domain with something special.

Figure 7.6 I'll bet they're glad they're at your site and no longer at that boring site.

Script 7.6 Use JavaScript to show surfers where they came from.

```
<HTML>
<HEAD>

<TITLE>Do you like me?</TITLE>

</HEAD>
<BODY BGCOLOR=WHITE>

<SCRIPT LANGUAGE=JAVASCRIPT>
 <!-- Hide script from old browsers

 if (document.referrer != "") {
    document.write("<H1>I hope you like this
    →page better than " + document.referrer
    →+ ".</H1>")
 }

 // End hiding script from old browsers -->
</SCRIPT>

</BODY>
</HTML>
```

JavaScript
and Cookies

In Web terms, a cookie is a unique nugget of information that a Web server gives to your browser when the two first meet and which they then share with each return visit. The remote server saves its part of the cookie and the information it contains about you; your browser does the same, as a plain text file stored on your computer's hard disk.

As a JavaScript author, you can do many useful things with cookies. If your site requires registration, you can set cookies to store your readers' user names and passwords, so they don't need to enter them every time they visit. You can keep track of which parts of your site the user has visited, and count the number of visits from that user.

There are many common misconceptions about cookies, so it's important to note what you can't do with them: you can't get any real information about the user such as their email address; you can't use cookies to check out the contents of their hard disks; and cookies can't transmit computer viruses. A cookie is just a simple text file on the user's hard disk where you the JavaScript programmer can store some information.

A cookie always includes the address of the server that sent it. That's the primary idea behind cookie technology: identification. Think of it as Caller ID for the Web, with variations on the theme—each Web site using cookies gives your browser a personalized ID of some sort, so that it can recognize you on the next visit. When you return to the Web server that first passed you a particular cookie, the server can query your browser to see if you are one of its many cookie holders. If so, the server can then retrieve the information stored in the cookie the two of you originally exchanged. Keep in mind that cookies just identify the computer being used, not the individual using the computer.

✔ Tip

- Wondering where those cookies are? Under Windows 95, Netscape Communicator keeps its cookies in c:\Program Files\Netscape\Users\ → <username>\cookies.txt. Previous version of Netscape used similar locations. Microsoft Internet Explorer 3.0 and later keeps the cookie jar in c:\Windows\Profiles\<username>\cookies\. On a Mac, the Netscape file is called MagicCookie, and it's in the Netscape folder inside the Preferences folder in the System Folder. Internet Explorer on the Mac stores its cookies in a file called Internet Preferences in the Preferences folder.

JAVASCRIPT AND COOKIES

Script 8.1 Setting a browser cookie.

```
<HTML>
<HEAD>

<TITLE>Set a cookie based on a form</TITLE>

<SCRIPT LANGUAGE=JAVASCRIPT>
 <!-- Hide script from older browsers
 expireDate = new Date
 expireDate.setYear(expireDate.getYear()+1)

 userName = ""
 if (document.cookie != "") {
   userName = document.cookie.split("=")[1]
 }

 function setCookie() {
   userName = document.myForm.nameField.value
   document.cookie =
   → "userName="+userName+";expires="
   →+ expireDate.toGMTString()
 }
 // End hiding script -->
</SCRIPT>

</HEAD>
<BODY BGCOLOR=WHITE>
 <FORM NAME=myForm><H1>
   Enter your name:<INPUT TYPE="text"
   →value="&{userName};"
   →name=nameField onBlur="setCookie()">
 </H1></FORM>

</BODY>
</HTML>
```

Figure 8.1 It doesn't look like much, but the content of the form's text field has just been written to a cookie.

Baking your first cookie

A cookie is a text string with a particular format, to wit:

cookieName=cookieValue;
expires=expirationDateGMT; path=URLpath;
domain=siteDomain

Breaking this down, the first part of the string gives the cookie a name and assigns it a value. This is the only mandatory part of a cookie; the rest of the string is optional. Next is the expiration date of the cookie; when this date is reached, the browser will automatically delete the cookie. The expiration date is followed by a URL path, which lets you store a URL in the cookie. Finally, you can store a domain value in the cookie.

Script 8.1 sets a cookie from a value entered by the user into a form. When you try this one out, it won't appear to do that much (as in Figure 8.1), but the cookie is actually being created. Later examples in this chapter build on this one.

To set a cookie:

1. expireDate = new Date

   First, you get the current date and put it into the variable expireDate.

2. expireDate.setYear(expireDate.getYear()+1)

   This line gets the year portion of expireDate, adds 1 to the year, then sets the year portion of expireDate to the new value.

3. userName = ""

   Next, you initialize the variable userName with a null value.

(Continued)

4. if (document.cookie != "") {
    userName = document.cookie.split("=")[1]
}

You begin a conditional test by first checking that the object document.cookie does not contain a null value. The method split ("=") splits a cookie record into fields, where cookieField[0] is the cookie name and cookieField[1] is the cookie value. Note that cookieField can be anything that you want to name a particular cookie's fields. So you assign userName the value returned by document.cookie.split("=")[1], that is, the cookie value.

5. function setCookie() {
    userName =
  → document.myForm.nameField.value

Now begin a new function, called setCookie(). The next line updates the value of userName with the result of the text field the user typed into.

6. document.cookie =
  → "userName="+userName+";expires="+
  → expireDate.toGMTString()
}

Here's where you write the cookie. You're setting document.cookie (remember, a cookie is just a text string, so you can use the same text string techniques to build it, like using the + sign to combine things) to contain the user's name and the cookie expiration date.

7. <FORM NAME=myForm><H1>
    Enter your name:<INPUT TYPE="text"
  → value="&{userName};" name=nameField
  → onBlur="setCookie()">

Finally, you need this HTML to set up and name the form and its field. The onBlur event handler (see Chapter 2) calls the setCookie function when the user leaves the text field.

A Fistful of Cookies

You can have multiple cookies on a page, and the format is:

"cookieName1=cookieValue1;
  → expires1=expirationDateGMT1;
  → path1=sitePath1;
  → domain1=siteDomain1";
"cookieName2=cookieValue2;
  → expires2=expirationDateGMT2;
  → path2=sitePath2;
  → domain2=siteDomain2"

Again, the only mandatory fields are the name and value pair.

The split(";") operator splits the multiple cookie record into an array, with each cookie in a cookie record numbered from 0 on. So cookieArray[0] would be the first cookie in the multiple cookie record, cookieArray[1] would be next, and so on. For more see the "Handling multiple cookies" example later in this chapter.

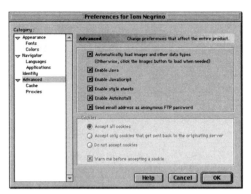

Figure 8.2 Netscape Communicator's cookie preference area.

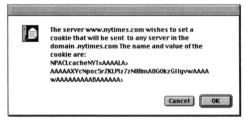

Figure 8.3 A typical cookie, sent to a browser from the *New York Times'* Web site.

✔ Tip

■ Set the Netscape preferences to show cookies being written out to get a better idea of what's happening behind the scenes. In Netscape Communicator, you'll find this preference in the Advanced section, as in Figure 8.2. After you do this, you'll get a dialog box that shows the value of the cookie as it is being set (Figure 8.3).

Reading a cookie

Once you've set a cookie, you'll need to retrieve it in order to do anything useful. The last example set the cookie with the text string "Tom." The very simple Script 8.2 shows you how to get that value from the cookie and display it on the screen (of course, you normally would not show off your cookies; this script just displays the cookie as an example).

To read a cookie:

1. if (document.cookie != "") {

First you make sure that the value in the object document.cookie isn't null.

2. document.write("Hello, "+
→ document.cookie.split("=")[1])
}

If the cookie isn't empty, then write a text string (the "Hello, " and note the extra space after the comma) and combine it with the split of the cookie value. You can see the result in Figure 8.4.

✔ Tip

■ Did you notice that you don't need to specify which of the cookies in the cookie file you are reading? That's because a cookie can only be read by the server that wrote it in the first place. The internal cookie mechanisms in the browser won't let you read or write cookies written by someone else. You'll only have access to your own cookies.

Script 8.2 This short script reads a previously set cookie and sends it to the document window.

```
<HTML>
<HEAD>

<TITLE>I know your name!</TITLE>

</HEAD>
<BODY BGCOLOR=WHITE>
<H1>
<SCRIPT LANGUAGE=JAVASCRIPT>
 <!-- Hide script from older browsers
 if (document.cookie != "") {
   document.write("Hello, "+
   →document.cookie.split("=")[1])
 }
 // End hiding script -->
</SCRIPT>
</H1>
</BODY>
</HTML>
```

Figure 8.4 This cookie had my name on it.

Script 8.3 This script counts your cookies.

```
<HTML>
<HEAD>

<TITLE>How many times have you been here before?
</TITLE>

<SCRIPT LANGUAGE=JAVASCRIPT>
  <!-- Hide script from older browsers
    expireDate = new Date
    expireDate.setYear(expireDate.getYear()+1)

  if (document.cookie == "") {
    hitCt = 0
  }
  else {
    hitCt = eval(document.cookie.split("=")[1])
  }

  hitCt++
  document.cookie = "pageHit="+hitCt+";expires="
→ + expireDate.toGMTString()
  // End hiding script -->
</SCRIPT>

</HEAD>
<BODY BGCOLOR=WHITE><H1>
<SCRIPT LANGUAGE=JAVASCRIPT>
  <!-- Hide script from older browsers
  document.write("You have visited this page "
→ + hitCt + " times.")
  // End hiding script -->
</SCRIPT></H1>
</BODY>
</HTML>
```

Using cookies as counters

Because cookies are persistent, that is, because they are available across multiple sessions between a Web server and browser, you can use cookies to store how many times a particular user has accessed a page. But this isn't the same thing as the page counters you see on many Web pages. Because a cookie is specific to a user, you can only tell that user how many times he or she has visited; you can't use cookies to tell all users how many times the page has been hit. Still, it's useful to know how to create such an individual counter, and you can adapt Script 8.3 for other purposes, too.

To use a cookie as a counter:

1. expireDate = new Date
   expireDate.setYear(expireDate.getYear()+1)

   These two lines are the same as in steps 1 and 2 of the "Baking your first cookie" example. Refer there for an explanation.

2. if (document.cookie == "") {
      hitCt = 0
   }

   This test checks to see if document.cookie contains a null value, and if so, the variable hitCt is set to 0.

3. else {
      hitCt = eval(document.cookie.split("=")[1])
   }

   If document.cookie is not null, then you read the cookie and set hitCt to the value of what's in the cookie. The eval command changes a text string (which is what is in the cookie) into a number (which is what the variable needs to use it as a counter).

4. hitCt++

   Now take the value of hitCt and add one to it, incrementing the counter.

   (Continued)

107

5. document.cookie =
→ "pageHit="+hitCt+";expires="
→ + expireDate.toGMTString()

This writes back the updated information to the cookie for future use. What's being written is a text string that combines the string "pageHit=" with the incremented value of hitCt, and adds "expires=" with the expiration date, which was incremented by one year back in step 1.

6. document.write("You have visited this page "
→ + hitCt + " times")

Note that this line is in the second script on the page. It writes the message to the user to the document window, as shown in Figure 8.5. There are extra spaces after "page" and before "times" to make the line look right on screen.

✔ Tips

■ It's possible that you'll get a JavaScript error message when you run Script 8.3; that's because the script isn't expecting there to be any cookies to begin with. If this happens to you, run Script 8.4, which deletes the cookies created by these examples, before you try out Script 8.3.

■ When you run this script, press the Reload button in your browser to see the counter increment.

■ You can adapt Script 8.3 for other purposes. One possibility would be to use a cookie to track when a particular user had last visited your site, and display different pages depending on when that was. For example, Microsoft's online magazine Slate (http://www.slate.com) has a cover page with some artwork and names of the stories in the day's issue. If the user visits the site more than once in a 24 hour period, they only see the cover page the first time; subsequent visits jump the user directly to the site's Table of Contents page.

Figure 8.5 Hard to believe that we've visited this dull page this often.

USING COOKIES AS COUNTERS

Script 8.4 This script deletes cookies.

```
script

<HTML>
<HEAD>

<TITLE>Delete those cookies</TITLE>

<SCRIPT LANGUAGE=JAVASCRIPT>
  <!-- Hide script from older browsers
  if (document.cookie != "") {
    if (confirm("Do you want to delete the
    →cookies?")) {
      thisCookie = document.cookie.split(";")
      expireDate = new Date
      expireDate.setYear(expireDate.getYear()-1)

      for (i=0; i<thisCookie.length; i++) {
        cookieName = thisCookie[i].split("=")[0]
        document.cookie = cookieName +
        →"=;expires=" + expireDate.toGMTString()
      }
      document.write("<H1>Number of cookies
      →deleted: " + thisCookie.length + "</H1>")
    }
  }
  // End hiding script -->
</SCRIPT>

</HEAD>
<BODY BGCOLOR=WHITE>

</BODY>
</HTML>
```

Figure 8.6 It's good interface design to confirm with the user whenever you are going to erase or delete anything.

Deleting cookies

At some point, you're going to want to delete a cookie or many cookies in a cookie record. It's fairly easy to do; one technique that works well is to simply set the cookie's expiration date to one year before the current date, which causes the browser to delete it automatically. Script 8.4 shows how to force your cookies to become stale.

To delete cookies:

1. if (document.cookie != "") {

   This test first checks to make sure that the cookie doesn't contain a null value, that is, the cookie record is not empty. If the test shows that the cookie is empty, then the script will do nothing.

2. if (confirm("Do you want to delete the → cookies?")) {

   This test is nested inside the last one, and tells the browser to put up a confirmation dialog box with the included text string (see Figure 8.6).

3. thisCookie = document.cookie.split(";")

   This line splits the content of the cookie record into an array with the split(";") operator and assigns it to the variable thisCookie.

4. expireDate = new Date
   expireDate.setYear(expireDate.getYear()-1)

   First get the current date and store it in expireDate. Then set the expiration date to the current year minus 1.

5. for (i=0; i<thisCookie.length; i++) {

   Now begin a for loop, so that you can delete all of the cookies, not just one. First set the value of i to 0, then as long as i is less than the number of cookies, increment i by 1.

(Continued)

6. cookieName = thisCookie[i].split("=")[0]

Use split("=")[0] to get the name of the particular cookie represented by the current value of i, then assign that name to the variable cookieName.

7. document.cookie = cookieName
→ + "=;expires=" + expireDate.toGMTString()
}

Here's where the cookie with the changed expiration date gets written back to disk.

8. document.write("<H1>Number of cookies
→ deleted: " + thisCookie.length + "</H1>")
    }
}

The script is out of the for loop now, and this line reports the number of cookies deleted to the document window, as seen in Figure 8.7.

Figure 8.7 Users should also get feedback that events have occurred as expected.

Script 8.5 Use an array to deal with multiple cookies in a single script.

```
████████████████ script ████████████████

<HTML>
<HEAD>

<TITLE>Handling more than one cookie</TITLE>

<SCRIPT LANGUAGE=JAVASCRIPT>
 <!-- Hide script from older browsers
 now = new Date
 expireDate = new Date
 expireDate.setYear(expireDate.getYear()+1)
 hitCt = 0
 lastVisit = ""

 if (document.cookie != "") {
   cookieArray = document.cookie.split(";")
   if (cookieArray[0] != "") {
     hitCt = eval(cookieArray[0].split("=")[1])
   }
   if (cookieArray[1] != "") {
     lastVisit = cookieArray[1].split("=")[1]
   }
 }

 hitCt++
 document.cookie = "pageHit="+hitCt+";expires="
 ↪+ expireDate.toGMTString()
 document.cookie = "pageVisit="+now+";expires="
 ↪+ expireDate.toGMTString()
 // End hiding script -->
</SCRIPT>

</HEAD>
<BODY BGCOLOR=WHITE><H1>
<SCRIPT LANGUAGE=JAVASCRIPT>
 <!-- Hide script from older browsers
 document.write("You have visited this page "
 ↪+ hitCt + " times.")
 if (lastVisit != "")
   document.write("<br>Your last visit was "
   ↪+ lastVisit)
 // End hiding script -->
</SCRIPT></H1>
</BODY>
</HTML>
```

Handling multiple cookies

You will often want to deal with more than one cookie at a time, and Script 8.5 shows you how to read from more than one cookie and display the information. This example shares a fair amount of code with the "Using cookies as counters" example.

To handle multiple cookies:

1. now = new Date
   expireDate = new Date
   expireDate.setYear(expireDate.getYear()+1)
   hitCt = 0
   lastVisit = ""

   These five lines initialize five variables in now-familiar ways.

2. if (document.cookie != "") {

   This test checks to see if document.cookie contains a null value.

3. cookieArray = document.cookie.split(";")

   Split up the cookie record into an array.

4. if (cookieArray[0] != "") {
       hitCt = eval(cookieArray[0].split("=")[1])
   }

   If the first item in the cookie array is not empty, then you read the cookie and set hitCt to the value of what's in the cookie.

5. if (cookieArray[1] != "") {
       lastVisit = cookieArray[1].split("=")[1]
       }
   }

   If the value of the second item in cookieArray is not null, then set the lastVisit variable to the value of what's in the cookie.

6. hitCt++

   This line increments the value of hitCt by 1.

   (Continued)

7. document.cookie =
→ "pageHit="+hitCt+";expires=" +
→ expireDate.toGMTString()
document.cookie =
→ "pageVisit="+now+";expires=" +
→ expireDate.toGMTString()

These two lines write the two cookies back to disk with an updated hit number and visit date.

8. document.write("You have visited this page "
→ + hitCt + " times.")

In the **BODY** script, this line writes the hit count cookie value to the screen, combined with some text.

9. if (lastVisit != "")
    document.write("
Your last visit was "
    → + lastVisit)

These lines check that lastVisit isn't null (in other words, the user has been here before), then writes a message to the user, followed by the lastVisit date.

✔ Tips

■ If you get a JavaScript error message when you run Script 8.5, it is again because the script isn't expecting there to be any cookies to begin with. If this happens to you, run Script 8.4, which deletes the cookies created by these examples, then run Script 8.5 again.

Figure 8.8 The two cookies, written to the screen (along with some other text).

HANDLING MULTIPLE COOKIES

JAVA AND PLUG-INS

As you've seen in previous chapters, JavaScript is a terrific tool to extend the range of things a browser can do. But as good as it is, JavaScript, like any scripting language, has limitations. It would be possible for a version of JavaScript to be created that would do virtually anything you could imagine, but it would be impractical because it would load the language down with possibly unneeded features, and performance would suffer. That's where Java applets and plug-ins enter the picture.

Java applets are programs that are downloaded to the user's browser, then run by the browser's Java interpreter. An applet can do many things that a JavaScript cannot; you can create entire applications in Java, with their own user interfaces.

Plug-ins are programs that extend the capabilities of the browser, usually to perform a specific function. Plug-ins are usually written in the C or C++ computer language for the best execution speed. Common plug-ins are Macromedia's Shockwave, which lets you view animations, and Apple's QuickTime plug-in, which allows the browser to play digital movies.

In this chapter, you'll learn how to use JavaScript to control Java applets and plug-ins.

Checking if Java is enabled

Before you call on a Java applet to enhance your page, you should check to see if the user even has a Java-enabled browser. You could try to infer Java capability by the version of the browser, but it's not a reliable indicator because most browsers that can use Java also offer the option of turning it off. So you want to use code which asks the browser if Java is turned on, or *enabled*. Script 9.1 shows you how to do it. As a side benefit, the script will also tell you if JavaScript is disabled.

To check if Java is enabled:

1. document.writeln("<H1>Java is ")

As you can see, there's no time wasted here; you start by writing the beginning of a text string into the document window, enclosed by the <H1> tag for emphasis.

2. if (!navigator.javaEnabled()) {

This test statement uses the navigator.javaEnabled() command, which does what you expect: it asks Navigator if Java is enabled. But here it is preceded by the ! operator, which means "not," so the statement asks "is Java not enabled?"

3. document.writeln("not ")
}

If the result of the test in step 2 is true (that is, Java is not enabled), then write the word "not "into the text string that is being built. Note the extra space after the word "not" which will ensure that the text string looks right.

Script 9.1 This script tells you whether the user has a Java-enabled browser.

```
<HTML>
<HEAD>

<TITLE>Do you have Java?</TITLE>
</HEAD>
<BODY BGCOLOR=WHITE>
<SCRIPT LANGUAGE=JAVASCRIPT>
 <!-- Hide script from old browsers

 document.writeln("<H1>Java is ")
 if (!navigator.javaEnabled()) {
    document.writeln("not ")
 }
 document.writeln("enabled.</H1>")

 // End hiding script from old browsers -->
</SCRIPT>
<NOSCRIPT>
 <H1>JavaScript is not enabled.</H1>
</NOSCRIPT>
</BODY>
</HTML>
```

Figure 9.1 As it turns out, this user's Java is hot and perking away.

4. document.writeln("enabled.</H1>")

If the script has gotten this far, then the test is false, and Java is enabled, so add text saying so to the text string, and close the <H1> tag. Figure 9.1 shows the result.

5. <NOSCRIPT>
<H1>JavaScript is not enabled.</H1>
</NOSCRIPT>

This is just plain HTML, but it is worth noting, as it tells the user that JavaScript isn't enabled.

✔ Tip

■ As with many of the other scripts in this book, you'll want to use Script 9.1 as part of your own scripts on a regular basis. It's always a good idea to build up a collection of scripts and script fragments that you can combine and assemble in many different ways in different scripts. If you find some way to organize these code fragments and make sure to label each one with a JavaScript comment (see Chapter 2 for more on using comments), you'll be far down the road when you go to create a new script.

Determining a user's IP address

It can be useful to know a user's IP address for a couple of reasons. First, it allows you to customize your content for certain users; for example, if you are working within a company which has an intranet (a company-wide network that uses Internet applications), you might want to have your Web page display one set of information to internal company users, and different information to people reaching the page from outside. Since your company will typically have a block of IP addresses, you can check if the user has one of those addresses. Another reason for checking IP addresses is to deny access to people with a given IP address, like from your company's bitter rivals.

Script 9.2, which because of variants in the JavaScript dialect only works in Netscape Communicator or Navigator (Internet Explorer users are left out), finds the user's IP address and displays it on screen. If the user is from Apple Computer, they get a special message. In the script, you'll see some software objects that begin with **java.net** followed by further description. These are Java objects, and it's important to type them in just as they appear. Explaining exactly what these objects do and how they work is outside of the scope of this book, but suffice it to say that putting these Java objects into the script allows JavaScript to call on Java to accomplish things that JavaScript can't do on its own.

Script 9.2 This script gets the user's IP address, and writes a special greeting to the screen if the user is from Apple Computer.

```
<HTML>
<HEAD>

<TITLE>Your IP address is</TITLE>
</HEAD>
<BODY BGCOLOR=WHITE>
<SCRIPT LANGUAGE=JAVASCRIPT>
 <!-- Hide script from old browsers

 browserName = navigator.appName
 browserVer = parseInt(navigator.appVersion)
 ipAdd = ""

 if (browserName == "Netscape" &&
 ⇥navigator.javaEnabled()) {
   if (browserVer >= 4) {
      ipAdd = java.net.InetAddress.getLocalHost().
      ⇥getHostName()
   }
   else {
      ipAdd = java.net.InetAddress.
      ⇥getLocalHostName()
   }
 }
 if (ipAdd != "") {
   document.writeln("<H1>Your IP address is: "
   ⇥+ ipAdd + ".</H1>")
   if (ipAdd.substring(0,7) == "17.254.") {
      document.write("<H2>Welcome, visitor from
      ⇥Apple!</H2>")
   }
 }

 // End hiding script from old browsers -->
</SCRIPT>
</BODY>
</HTML>
```

To determine a user's IP address:

1. browserName = navigator.appName

The first line sets browserName to navigator.appName, the name of the browser.

2. browserVer = parseInt(navigator.appVersion)
ipAdd = ""

The first part of this sets the variable browserVer to be the integer portion of the version number of the user's browser. The next part initializes the variable ipAdd.

3. if (browserName == "Netscape" &&
→ navigator.javaEnabled( )) {

This line starts a conditional statement and says that if browserName is "Netscape" and the result of the navigator.javaEnabled object is true, then continue to the next line.

4. if (browserVer >= 4) {
ipAdd = java.net.InetAddress.getLocalHost().
→ getHostName()
}

This test first checks if the value of browserVer is 4 or greater. If so, the browser is Navigator 4.0 or later, and it can handle the next line, which uses a Java method to ask the user's browser to send the user's IP address.

5. else {
    ipAdd = java.net.InetAddress.
→ getLocalHostName()
    }
}

If the browser is earlier than Navigator 4, then use this different form of the Java method.

6. if (ipAdd != " ") {

If the script has gotten this far and the value of ipAdd is not empty, then continue on with the script.

(*Continued*)

7. document.writeln("<H1>Your IP address is: "
→ + ipAdd + ".</H1>")

This line writes the IP address into the
document window, as in Figure 9.2.

8. if (ipAdd.substring(0,7) == "17.254.") {
   document.write("<H2>Welcome, visitor
→ from Apple!</H2>")
   }
}

This is where the script checks to see
if the visitor is from Apple Computer.
Apple has a IP address block which starts
with 17.254., so the script tests the value
of ipAdd to see if it begins with those
characters. That's what the substring(0,7)
part is about. If the value matches, then
the script writes in the special greeting,
as seen in Figure 9.3.

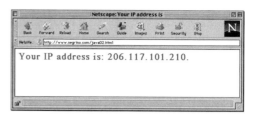

Figure 9.2 The usual result just gives the user's IP
address.

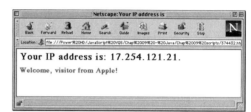

Figure 9.3 If the user is browsing from Apple, they get
something special.

Script 9.3 When you need to discover the user's screen size, this script gets the job done.

```
========== script ==========
<HTML>
<HEAD>

<TITLE>Let's open a big window!</TITLE>
</HEAD>
<BODY BGCOLOR=WHITE>
<SCRIPT LANGUAGE=JAVASCRIPT>
 <!-- Hide script from old browsers

 sWidth = 0
 sHeight = 0

 if (navigator.appName == "Netscape" &&
 →navigator.javaEnabled()) {
   sWidth = java.awt.Toolkit.
   →getDefaultToolkit().
   →getScreenSize().width
   sHeight = java.awt.Toolkit.
   →getDefaultToolkit().
   →getScreenSize().height
 }
 if (sWidth == 0 || sHeight == 0) {
   sWidth = 640
   sHeight = 480
 }
 document.writeln("<H1>Your screen dimensions
 →are: " + sWidth + " x " + sHeight + ".</H1>")
 newWin = window.open("","newWin","width=" +
 →sWidth + ",height=" + sHeight)

 // End hiding script from old browsers -->
</SCRIPT>
</BODY>
</HTML>
```

Getting the user's monitor size

If you plan to open up windows on the user's screen, the screen size is a nice bit of information to have. Using Java, you can get the size of a user's screen, then you can use that information in other parts of your script. Script 9.3 discovers the screen size, writes the size in the current browser window, then creates a new window to the full screen size.

To get the user's screen size:

1. sWidth = 0
   sHeight = 0

   First, you need to initialize the variables that will hold the screen width and screen size with a zero value.

2. if (navigator.appName == "Netscape" &&
   → navigator.javaEnabled()) {

   This is the same conditional as in the previous example. If the user is using Navigator and Java is enabled, then forge onward.

3. sWidth = java.awt.Toolkit.
   → getDefaultToolkit().
   → getScreenSize().width

   This line isn't pretty, but all it does is use a Java method to discover the user's screen width (in pixels) and put that number into the sWidth variable.

4. sHeight = java.awt.Toolkit.
   → getDefaultToolkit().
   → getScreenSize().height
   }

   This line does the same thing as step 3, but with the screen height and the sHeight variable.

(Continued)

5. if (sWidth == 0 || sHeight == 0) {

This tests to see if either variable still contains 0. If so, then using Java to query the screen size failed for some mysterious reason (see the Tip below).

6. sWidth = 640
sHeight = 480
}

If the script couldn't get the screen size from Java, you'll just have to set it yourself to a default size of 640 by 480.

7. document.writeln("<H1>Your screen
→ dimensions are: " + sWidth + " x "
→ + sHeight + "."</H1>)

This line writes the values of the variables, plus some extra text, to the document window. See Figure 9.4.

8. newWin = window.open("","newWin",
→ "width=" + sWidth + ",height=" + sHeight)

Finally, take the values of the sWidth and sHeight variables and use them to create a new window using the window.open command. See Chapter 6 for more about working with windows.

✔ Tip

■ When you do a test using Java, the test may fail for any number of reasons, not the least being that the current implementations of Java aren't very stable. You should always build into your scripts the possibility that the Java won't work, and keep your scripts from crashing and burning if Java lets you down.

Figure 9.4 The screen dimensions shown here were passed to JavaScript from a Java method.

GETTING THE USER'S MONITOR SIZE

Script 9.4 In order to gain a bit more control over text display, this script passes text from JavaScript to a Java applet.

```
script

<HTML>
<HEAD>

<TITLE>Write to Java</TITLE>
<SCRIPT LANGUAGE=JAVASCRIPT>
 <!-- Hide script from old browsers

   function startUp() {
     document.myApplet.newText(prompt("What do
   →you want to say?",""))
   }

 // End hiding script from old browsers -->
</SCRIPT>
</HEAD>
<BODY onload="startUp()">
 <APPLET CODE='WriteIt.class'
 →WIDTH=600 HEIGHT=50 NAME=myApplet>
 </APPLET>
</BODY>
</HTML>
```

Script 9.5 This example isn't JavaScript at all; it's the Java source code for the Java applet we're calling in Script 9.4.

```
applet

import java.applet.*;
import java.awt.*;

public class writeIt extends Applet {
 Font f = new Font("TimesRoman",Font.BOLD,36);
 String whatToSay;

 public void paint(Graphics g) {
   g.setFont(f);
   g.drawString(this.whatToSay, 100 , 25);
 }

 public void newText(String s) {
   this.whatToSay = s;
   repaint();
 }

}
```

Figure 9.5 Here's the JavaScript dialog box that accepts the user's input.

Using Java to display text

HTML doesn't have a lot of control over text in terms of font face and size, and neither does Java, but there are some built-in fonts in Java that you can access. Script 9.4 uses a JavaScript dialog to prompt the user for a text string, then passes the string to Java, which displays it in 36 point bold Times Roman. If you're curious, you can see the Java source code in Script 9.5.

To use Java to display text:

1. function startUp() {

   This line just begins the function startUp.

2. document.myApplet.newText
   → (prompt("What do you want to say?",""))

   This software object is best read from right to left. It enters a text string with the query for the user, and the prompt command makes that text string appear in a JavaScript dialog box (see Figure 9.5). The result of the prompt (that is, the user's entry) will go into the document.myApplet.newText object. Note that myApplet is the name of the Java applet that will do the work of displaying the user's text. Look in step 4 below to where the name myApplet is assigned.

3. <BODY onload="startUp()">

   To the usual HTML BODY tag, you need to add the startUp function to trigger when the page is loaded. Figure 9.6 shows the result.

4. <APPLET CODE='WriteIt.class' WIDTH=600
   → HEIGHT=50 NAME=myApplet>
   </APPLET>

   More HTML, this line uses the APPLET tag to specify the name of the code file, the size in pixels, and the name of the Java applet.

✔ Tips

■ This example doesn't do any wrapping of text or check to see that the text entered in the JavaScript prompt dialog will fit on the screen. Excess text simply runs off the right edge of the screen. If you use this code, you should replace step 2 with code that checks the length of the newText string, and wraps or truncates it appropriately. One way to do this would be to add an if test that gets the length of the document.myApplet.newText string, and pops up a dialog if the user exceeds the maximum permitted length. For example, lets say that you've determined while testing the script that you can only use a string of 20 characters before it passes off the right edge of the screen. These lines would do the trick:

```
tempText=prompt("What do you want to
→ say?", "")
if (tempText.length > 20) {
    alert ("You may only type in a maximum
    → of 20 characters.")
    startUp()
}
else {
    document.myApplet.newText(tempText)
}
```

■ There are three font types you can access that are built into every Java virtual machine. These three font types are Serif, Sans Serif, and Mono. The reason I call these font types instead of just fonts is that in order to work reliably on any computer, the VM maps the three font types to the fonts that actually exist on the computer on which it is running. On most computers they map to Times Roman, Helvetica, and Courier, respectively.

Figure 9.6 This is the styled text produced by the Java applet. Unlike HTML, the Java lets you specify a real font, font size, and style.

The Java Virtual Machine

A Java virtual machine, abbreviated as VM, is the Java interpreter that comes with browsers that takes applets and runs them. Java virtual machines are now increasingly being built into operating systems such as the Mac OS with the Macintosh Runtime for Java, and similar virtual machines for the various flavors of Microsoft Windows.

Script 9.6 JavaScript can make use of the Netscape LiveAudio plug-in.

```
                    script
<HTML>
<HEAD>
<TITLE>Sound controller</TITLE>
<SCRIPT LANGUAGE=JAVASCRIPT>
 <!-- Hide script from old browsers

 function startSound() {
   document.mySound.play(false)
 }

 function pauseSound() {
   document.mySound.pause()
 }

 function stopSound() {
   document.mySound.stop()
 }

 function changeVol(changeBy) {
   currentVol = document.mySound.GetVolume()
   if (currentVol < 100 && currentVol > 0) {
     document.mySound.setvol(currentVol+changeBy)
   }
 }

 // End hiding script from old browsers -->
</SCRIPT>
</HEAD>

<BODY BGCOLOR=WHITE>

<EMBED SRC="jurassic.wav" NAME="mySound"
 →MASTERSOUND AUTOSTART=NO HIDDEN=TRUE>
<CENTER><H1>Sound Controls</H1>
<FORM>
 <INPUT TYPE="button" VALUE="Vol +"
 →onClick="javascript:changeVol(10)">
 <INPUT TYPE="button" VALUE="Vol -"
 →onClick="javascript:changeVol(-10)">
 <INPUT TYPE="button" VALUE="Start"
 →onClick="javascript:startSound()">
 <INPUT TYPE="button" VALUE="Pause"
 →onClick="javascript:pauseSound()">
 <INPUT TYPE="button" VALUE="Stop"
 →onClick="javascript:stopSound()">

</FORM>
</CENTER>
</BODY>
</HTML>
```

Playing sounds using a plug-in

Now, let's turn from Java to plug-ins. In this example, you'll use Netscape's LiveAudio plug-in to play a sound file. You'll also create control buttons (using an HTML form) that start, pause, and stop the sound, and increase or decrease the volume. Script 9.6 contains several functions that handle the control functions. See Figure 9.7 for the playback.

To play sounds using the LiveAudio plug-in:

1. function startSound() {
   document.mySound.play(false)
   }

   This function plays the sound. The false parameter tells the script not to loop the sound, that is, only to play the sound once.

2. function pauseSound() {
   document.mySound.pause()
   }

   This function tells the document to pause the playing of the sound mySound.

3. function stopSound() {
   document.mySound.stop()
   }

   This function tells the document to stop playing mySound.

4. function changeVol(changeBy) {

   The function changeVol receives the value of the variable changeBy.

5. currentVol = document.mySound.GetVolume()

   This line just gets the value of the sound volume from the document and puts it into currentVol.

   (Continued)

6. if (currentVol < 100 && currentVol > 0) {

This conditional test looks to see if the value of currentVol is less than 100 (the maximum value) and greater than 0 (the minimum value).

7. document.mySound.setvol
→ (currentVol+changeBy)
   }
}

If the value of currentVol isn't already at the maximum or minimum, change it by the value of changeBy, which is either +10 units or −10 units, depending on whether the user has pressed the Vol + or Vol − buttons.

8. <EMBED SRC="jurassic.wav"
→ NAME="mySound" MASTERSOUND
→ AUTOSTART=NO HIDDEN=TRUE>

The HTML EMBED tag needs several bits of information. The SRC attribute gives EMBED the name of the sound file. NAME provides a file name or URL of the sound for the JavaScript to use. MASTERSOUND is a required attribute whenever you use a named sound. Setting AUTOSTART to NO means that the sound won't start by itself when the page is loaded. And setting HIDDEN to TRUE makes sure that LiveAudio doesn't display its own built-in control panel (since we've created a custom panel).

9. <INPUT TYPE="button" VALUE="Vol +"
→ onClick="javascript:changeVol(10)">

This is the first of five lines that set up the form's control buttons (look to Script 9.6 for the rest; they all work in the same way). This particular line sets up the Vol + button and triggers the JavaScript changeVol function when the user clicks the button. The 10 is the value that gets assigned to the changeBy variable in step 4 above.

Figure 9.7 A custom sound control panel, using form buttons.

More about LiveAudio

In the example above, Netscape calls LiveAudio because that's what's specified in the browser for .wav files under helper applications. LiveAudio automatically knows about 15 methods, with the following syntax:

play({loop[TRUE, FALSE or an INT]},
→ '{url_to_play}') pause()

stop()

StopAll()

start_time({number of seconds})

end_time({number of seconds})

setvol({percentage number – without "%" sign})

fade_to({volume percent you wish to
→ fade to – without the "%" sign})

fade_from_to({volume percent start fade},
→ {volume percent end fade})

start_at_beginning()

stop_at_end()

IsReady()

IsPlaying()

IsPaused()

GetVolume()

These methods are referenced by giving the EMBED tag a NAME attribute, then calling document.embedName.method(), where method() is one of the methods above.

Script 9.7 Rollovers can trigger plug-ins using JavaScript.

```
script
<HTML>
<HEAD>
<TITLE>Rollover Sound</TITLE>
<SCRIPT LANGUAGE=JAVASCRIPT>
 <!-- Hide script from old browsers

 function playSound(SName) {
   if (document.embeds[SName] != null &&
   →document.embeds[SName].IsReady()) {
     document.embeds[SName].play(false);
   }
 }

 // End hiding script from old browsers -->
</SCRIPT>
</HEAD>

<BODY BGCOLOR=WHITE>

<CENTER><H1>Sounds on rollovers</H1></CENTER>
<p><A HREF=javascript:void("")
OnMouseover="playSound('moof')"><IMG
 →SRC='dogcow.gif' WIDTH=43 HEIGHT=34 BORDER=0
 →ALIGN=LEFT HSPACE=30></A>
<H3>If you pet Clarus she will moof for you!</H3>
<EMBED SRC="moof.au" NAME="moof" HIDDEN=TRUE
 →LOOP=FALSE AUTOSTART=FALSE MASTERSOUND>
</BODY>
</HTML>
```

Figure 9.8 When you pet the dogcow, she will moof for you!

Playing a sound on a rollover

You learned about rollovers back in Chapter 3 when you worked with images. But you can also use rollovers to trigger plug-ins. In Script 9.7 you'll learn how to make a rollover play a sound with the LiveAudio plug-in, as in Figure 9.8

To play a sound on a rollover:

1. function playSound(SName) {

   The function playSound receives the value of the variable SName.

2. if (document.embeds[SName] != null &&
   → document.embeds[SName].IsReady()) {

   This line tests to see if the embedded object, in this case, the sound file from the EMBED tag at the end of Script 9.7 is not null (the sound file exists) and if the sound is ready and available to be played.

3. document.embeds[SName].play(false);
   }

   If the sound is ready, then this line plays it. Again, the false parameter makes sure that the sound only plays once.

4. <A HREF=javascript:void("")
   → OnMouseover="playSound('moof')">
   → <IMG SRC='dogcow.gif' WIDTH=43
   → HEIGHT=34 BORDER=0 ALIGN=LEFT
   → HSPACE=30></A>

   The javascript:void("") tells the anchor tag not to link to another HTML page. When the user moves the mouse over the linked image, the sound moof gets played. The IMG tag specifies the image to be rolled over. The remaining EMBED tag in the script works the same as in the previous example.

About the Dogcow

The mythical animal we have used in this example is the dogcow, beloved mascot of Apple Computer's Developer Technical Support engineers. The origin of the dogcow is shrouded in mystery (sort of), but dedicated researchers in Dogcattle Studies have determined a few salient facts:

- It doesn't look quite like either a dog or a cow. Therefore the name.
- The sound a dogcow makes is "Moof!"
- The dogcow's name is Clarus. Yes, spelled differently than the software company.
- More information on the pedigree of the dogcow can be found at http://devworld.apple.com/dev/dts/dogcow.html

ABOUT THE DOGCOW

JavaScript and Cascading Style Sheets

CSS-enabled browsers

As of Fall 1997, the only browsers that support Cascading Style Sheets are Microsoft Internet Explorer version 4, Netscape Communicator version 4, and Netscape Navigator version 4 for all of their supported computer platforms.

It's also important to note that each company's browser implements the CSS "standard" in different ways, virtually guaranteeing that style sheets you implement with one browser in mind won't work as intended when viewed by users with the other company's browser.

A recent addition to the newer browsers is Cascading Style Sheets (CSS). CSS is the technique wherein a page can have "styles," that is, if all the text in your <H1> tags are red and in font face Palatino, CSS will let you set that up once, and then all following <H1> tags on that page will automatically be formatted correctly. Because CSS is so new, different browsers implement it in different ways. There is a CSS standard, though, which can be found at http://www.w3.org/Style/css/. For more about CSS and HTML, refer to *HTML for the World Wide Web: Visual QuickStart Guide* by Elizabeth Castro, available from Peachpit Press.

Unfortunately, at the time of this writing there is no standard for the use of JavaScript with CSS. Both Netscape and Microsoft have implemented their own mutually incompatible versions of how JavaScript should refer to style sheets.

This chapter will show a little of what can be done with today's browsers. Once a standard has been agreed upon, expect the next version of each of the browsers to be compliant. You can find out more about proposed standards at http://www.w3.org/DOM/.

Moving an object
(Netscape Communicator and Navigator only)

The first thing you need to know about styles and JavaScript is that CSS styles are accessible as JavaScript objects. An object can be placed on a page in a precise location using CSS, and then JavaScript can be added to animate that object. In this example, as shown in Script 10.1, we declare three styles: leftfore, which sets up the left foreground object; mover, which sets up the object we are going to animate; and rightfore, the style of the right foreground object.

Script 10.1 This script shows how to move an object across the page.

```
                        script
<HTML>
<HEAD>

<TITLE>Moon</TITLE>

<SCRIPT LANGUAGE=JAVASCRIPT>
 <!-- Hide script from older browsers

 function slide() {
   document.mover.left+=2;
   if (document.mover.left < 470) {
     setTimeout("slide()",20)
   }
 }

 // End hiding script -->
</SCRIPT>

<STYLE TYPE="text/css">
 #leftfore {position: absolute; left: 0; top: 5;
 'z-Index: 2;}
 #mover {position: absolute; left: 5; top: 5;
 'z-Index: 1;}
 #rightfore {position: absolute; left: 470;
 →top: 5; z-Index: 2;}
</STYLE>

</HEAD>
<BODY BGCOLOR=BLACK onLoad="slide()">

 <DIV ID="leftfore"><IMG SRC="img/black_dot.gif"
 'WIDTH="250" HEIGHT="250"></DIV>
 <DIV ID="mover"><IMG SRC="img/full_moon.jpg"
 'WIDTH="232" HEIGHT="232"></DIV>
 <DIV ID="rightfore"><IMG SRC="img/black_dot.gif"
 'WIDTH="250" HEIGHT="250"></DIV>

</BODY>
</HTML>
```

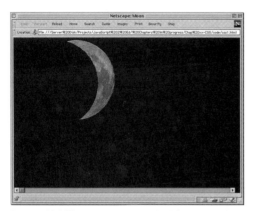

Figure 10.1 The moon starts on the left, shadowed behind the foreground object…

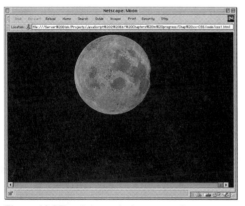

Figure 10.2 Travels towards the center where it can be seen in its entirety…

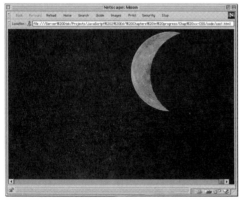

Figure 10.3 Then ends up on the right, where it is again shadowed by a foreground object.

To move a CSS object:

1. function slide() {

Create a function named slide.

2. document.mover.left+=2

This line moves the left side of everything with the style mover over two pixels, as shown in Figures 10.1, 10.2, and 10.3.

3. if (document.mover.left < 470) {
        setTimeout("slide()",20)
        }
   }

If the move has put the left side of the object with the style mover in the left-most 470 pixels of the window, use setTimeout to wait 20 milliseconds and run slide again.

✔ Tips

- Each style in this example includes a z-Index. The object with the higher-numbered z-Index is shown when two objects occupy the same space.

- This style of JavaScript with CSS only works with Netscape. Browser detection of some sort should be used on scripts like these, as described in Chapter 2.

MOVING AN OBJECT

Moving CSS text
(Netscape Communicator and Navigator only)

Cascading Style Sheets treat text like just another kind of object. Script 10.2 shows an example of text that moves diagonally down across the page.

To move CSS text in Netscape:

1. function moveIt() {

Create a function called moveIt.

2. document.mover.top+=2
document.mover.left+=2

Move any objects (text, in this case) with the style mover down 2 pixels and over 2 pixels by moving the top and left edges. Figure 10.4 shows the text traveling down the page.

3. if (document.mover.top <=
→ (window.innerHeight-10)) {
   setTimeout("moveIt()",20)
   }
}

If the top-most pixel of the moving area is not within 10 pixels of the bottom of the window, use setTimeout to wait 20 milliseconds and execute moveIt again.

✔ Tips

■ The window.innerHeight variable shown above is a JavaScript 1.2 variable set by Netscape browsers. It gives you the height of the inner part of the window, between the menu bar and the status bar.

■ Again, this script only works in Netscape. The following script shows how to move text in Internet Explorer.

Script 10.2: This script (for Netscape only) moves the text down and to the right.

```
<HTML>
<HEAD>
<TITLE>Watch me go!</TITLE>
<SCRIPT>
 <!-- Hide script from older browsers

 function moveIt() {
   document.mover.top+=2
   document.mover.left+=2
   if (document.mover.top <=
   → (window.innerHeight-10)) {
     setTimeout("moveIt()",20)
   }
 }

 // End hiding script -->
</SCRIPT>
<STYLE TYPE="text/css">
 #mover {position: absolute; left: 5; top: 5;
 →font-size:36pt;}
</STYLE>
</HEAD>
<BODY BGCOLOR="WHITE" onLoad="moveIt()">

 <DIV ID="mover">On the road again...</DIV>

</BODY>
</HTML>
```

Figure 10.4 Watch that text move!

Script 10.3 This script (for MSIE only) moves the text over and to the right.

```
<HTML>
<HEAD>
<title>Watch me go!</title>
<SCRIPT LANGUAGE=JAVASCRIPT>
 <!-- Hide script from older browsers

 function moveIt() {
   if (document.all) {
     document.all.mover.style.pixelTop+=2
     document.all.mover.style.pixelLeft+=2
     setTimeout("moveIt()",20)
   }
 }

 // End hiding script -->
</SCRIPT>
<STYLE TYPE="text/css">
 #mover {position: absolute; left: 5; top: 5;
 →font-size:36pt;}
</STYLE>
</HEAD>
<BODY BGCOLOR="WHITE" onload="moveIt()">

 <DIV ID="mover">On the road again...</DIV>

</BODY>
</HTML>
```

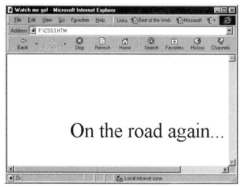

Figure 10.5 And watch it go!

Moving CSS text
(Internet Explorer only)

Cascading Style Sheets treat text like just another kind of object. Script 10.3 for Internet Explorer shows an example of text that moves diagonally down across the page.

To move CSS text in Internet Explorer:

1. function moveIt() {

   Create a function called moveIt.

2.   if (document.all) {

   Verify that the user is running Internet Explorer by checking to see if document.all is valid. This is how IE refers to CSS objects.

3.   document.all.mover.style.pixelTop+=2
       document.all.mover.style.pixelLeft+=2

   Move any objects (text, in this case) with the style mover down 2 pixels and over 2 pixels by moving the top and left edges. Figure 10.5 shows the text traveling down the page.

4.   setTimeout("moveIt()",20)
       }
     }

   Use setTimeout to wait 20 milliseconds and execute moveIt again.

✔ Tip

■ Note the differences between how Netscape and Internet Explorer handle CSS objects in JavaScript. While Script 10.3 and Script 10.2 have identical results, the code that does the actual work is quite different.

Modifying a CSS drop shadow

(Internet Explorer only)

There are very few modifications you can make to CSS objects with JavaScript in Netscape. Internet Explorer, on the other hand, has a data type called filters, which allows JavaScript access to many ways to modify objects. Script 10.4 shows the use of the drop shadow filter (called dropShadow) to modify text appearance. The drop shadow starts 50 pixels over and down from the original text, and then moves closer and closer until they overlap (Figure 10.6).

To modify a drop shadow:

1. function doDrop(xCoord, yCoord) {

   Create a function named doDrop, and pass in two variables: the current x and y coordinates of the drop shadow.

2. if (document.all && xCoord > 1) {

   If the user is browsing with IE and the x coordinate passed in is greater than one, do the following steps.

3. xCoord -= 1
   yCoord -= 1

   Subtract one from both the x and y coordinates to bring the dropShadow in closer to the original.

4. document.all.dropText.style.filter="dropShadow
   → (offX=" + xCoord+ ", offY=" + yCoord + ")"

   Reset the filter style of the dropText object to the new value of dropShadow, by setting the x offset (offX) to the x coordinate (xCoord) and the y offset (offY) to the y coordinate (yCoord).

5. setTimeout("doDrop(" + xCoord + ","
   → + yCoord + ")", 100)
      }
   }

   Use setTimeout to wait 100 milliseconds and then call doDrop again with the newly revised x and y coordinates.

Script 10.4 Use Internet Explorer's drop shadow filter with JavaScript to move the drop shadow on this text.

```
<HTML>
<HEAD>
<TITLE>Drop it!</TITLE>

<SCRIPT LANGUAGE=JAVASCRIPT>
  <!-- Hide script from older browsers

  function doDrop(xCoord, yCoord) {
    if (document.all && xCoord > 1) {
      xCoord -= 1
      yCoord -= 1
      document.all.dropText.style.filter=
      →"dropShadow(offX=" + xCoord+ ",
      →offY=" + yCoord + ")"
      setTimeout("doDrop(" + xCoord + "," +
      →yCoord + ")", 100)
    }
  }

  // End hiding script -->
</SCRIPT>
<STYLE>
  #dropText {width:420; height:100; font-size:36pt;
  →filter:dropShadow(offX=50,offY=50)}
</STYLE>
</HEAD>
<BODY BGCOLOR="WHITE" onLoad="doDrop(50,50)">

  <DIV ID="dropText">Drop it!</DIV>

</BODY>
</HTML>
```

Figure 10.6 Move the drop shadow closer and closer to the original text.

Script 10.5 This script uses CSS and JavaScript to rotate a shadow around a block of text.

```
script

<HTML>
<HEAD>
<TITLE>Shadow it!</TITLE>

<SCRIPT LANGUAGE=JAVASCRIPT>
 <!-- Hide script from older browsers

 function doShadow(newDirection) {
   if (document.all && newDirection< 360) {
     newDirection += 10
     document.all.dropText.style.filter=
     →"shadow(direction=" + newDirection + ")"
     setTimeout("doShadow(" + newDirection + ")",
     →100)
   }
 }

 // End hiding script -->
</SCRIPT>
<STYLE>
 #dropText {width:500; height:100;
 →font-size:36pt; filter:shadow(direction=90)}
</STYLE>
</HEAD>
<BODY BGCOLOR="WHITE" onLoad="doShadow(90)">

 <DIV ID="dropText">Me and my shadow...</DIV>

</BODY>
</HTML>
```

Figure 10.7 The shadow is down and to the right...

Figure 10.8 And now the shadow is up and to the left.

Rotating a CSS shadow
(Internet Explorer only)

Script 10.5 shows the use of the shadow filter to modify text appearance. In this example, the shadow starts at 90 degrees from the original text and then circles around to 360 degrees.

To rotate a shadow:

1. function doShadow(newDirection) {

Create a new function, doShadow, which is passed newDirection, the current direction of the shadow.

2. if (document.all && newDirection < 360) {

If the user is browsing with IE and newDirection is less than 360 (the maximum number of degrees) then do the next steps.

3. newDirection += 10
document.all.dropText.style.filter=
→ "shadow(direction=" + newDirection + ")"

Add 10 degrees to newDirection, to set the new location of the shadow, and set up the filter with the new shadow values, moving the drop shadow as shown in Figures 10.7 and 10.8.

4. setTimeout("doShadow(" + newDirection
→ + ")", 100)
}
}

Use setTimeout to wait 100 milliseconds, and call doShadow again with the current value of newDirection.

Modifying a CSS glow
(Internet Explorer only)

Script 10.6 shows the use of the glow filter to modify text appearance. In this example, the glow starts with a glow strength of 5 and works its way up to the maximum glow strength of 255, as shown in Figures 10.9 and 10.10.

To modify a CSS glow:

1. function doGlow(newStrength) {

   Create a new function named doGlow, which is passed newStrength, the current glow strength.

2. if (document.all && newStrength < 255) {

   Check to see that the browser being used is Internet Explorer and the current glow strength is less than the maximum of 255, then do the following.

3. newStrength += 10
   document.all.glowText.style.filter=
   → "glow(strength=" + newStrength+ ")"

   Increase the strength of the glow by 10, and reset the filter style of the glow object to the new value of newStrength.

4. setTimeout("doGlow(" + newStrength+ ")",
   → 100)
      }
   }

   Use setTimeout to wait 100 milliseconds, then call doGlow again with the new glow strength value.

Script 10.6 This script creates a glow that increases around the text.

```
<HTML>
<HEAD>
<TITLE>I'm radioactive!</TITLE>

<SCRIPT LANGUAGE=JAVASCRIPT>
 <!-- Hide script from older browsers

 function doGlow(newStrength) {
   if (document.all && newStrength < 255) {
   newStrength += 10
     document.all.glowText.style.filter=
     → "glow(strength=" + newStrength+ ")"
     setTimeout("doGlow(" + newStrength+ ")",
     → 100)
     }
 }

 // End hiding script -->
</SCRIPT>
<STYLE>
 #glowText {width:500; height:100;
 → font-size:36pt; filter:glow(strength=5)}
</STYLE>
</HEAD>
<BODY BGCOLOR="WHITE" onLoad="doGlow(5)">

 <CENTER><DIV ID="glowText">
 → I'm glowing...</DIV></CENTER>

</BODY>
</HTML>
```

Figure 10.9 The glow starts out relatively small around the text...

Figure 10.10 then the glow steadily increases in strength.

DEBUGGING
YOUR JAVASCRIPT

It's often said that 90% of the time you spend writing programs is actually spent debugging them—that is, making them work after they've been written. Add to this the sad fact that none of the browsers that support JavaScript show meaningful error messages, and you have a recipe for frustration. This chapter will show some of the most common JavaScript errors, how to identify them, how to fix them, and how you can avoid them in the first place.

Netscape's built-in debugger

Netscape's browser has a built in debugger that can be accessed from any browser window.

To use Netscape's debugger:

1. In the location field of the browser, enter javascript:.

A page will appear, with two frames. The lower frame has a text field where you enter your JavaScript text.

✔ Tips

- Multiple JavaScript lines can be entered in the single text field by separating them with semicolons.

- Be sure to enter the colon after "javascript:" in the location field, or the browser will try to find http://www.javascript.com/.

- In addition to using the keyword javascript: to bring up this window, you can also use the words mocha: or livescript: (early names for JavaScript).

Figure 11.1 Verifying the syntax of alert by trying it in Netscape's built-in debugger.

Why is it called "Debugging"?

In 1951 Grace Hopper was a programmer working on the UNIVAC I, the first large-scale computer. One day, a system that had been working suddenly stopped. She researched the problem and was able to find the cause—a moth inside the computer. She pasted the "bug" inside the system logbook, and computer problems have been called bugs ever since.

Grace Hopper was born in 1906, earned a Ph.D. from Yale in Math & Physics in 1934, served in the Navy off and on from 1943 to 1986 (retiring as a Rear Admiral), and passed away in 1992. She was one of the pioneers of programming.

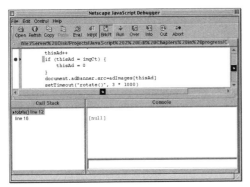

Figure 11.2 Running a script with the Netscape JavaScript Debugger.

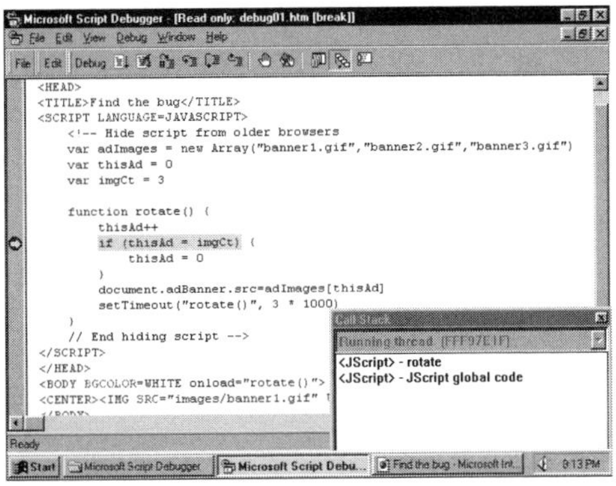

Figure 11.3 Viewing the same script in the Microsoft Script Debugger.

JavaScript debuggers

Both Netscape and Microsoft provide separate, more full-featured debuggers that run with their browsers. Netscape offers the Netscape JavaScript Debugger, a Java applet that runs inside Netscape Communicator. Microsoft has the Microsoft Script Debugger, a separate program that requires Internet Explorer to work. You can download each from the Web sites of their respective makers.

✔ Tips

- As of this writing, both debuggers are still in beta testing. This means that while they are available for download, it's likely that they still have a number of bugs. Read the accompanying documentation carefully before trying either program.

- Both debuggers let you set breakpoints, which allow you to stop the script processing at given points. This can allow you to check on the value of variables at any given point.

- The Microsoft Script Debugger only works on Internet Explorer 3.02 or later, on Windows 95 or NT systems only. The Netscape JavaScript Debugger works only with Communicator, on Windows 95, NT, Mac PowerPC, and several varieties of UNIX.

JAVASCRIPT DEBUGGERS

Common errors

There are a number of common errors, and browsers only give you small hints as to their causes. Here are some of the ones you're likely to run into, with their error messages. Script 11.1 shows the completely debugged version of the script.

To debug your script, look for these gotcha's:

■ Wherever you compare two fields to see if they're equal, your script must have two equal signs, i.e., "==" (Script 11.2). The error message that will appear is shown in Figure 11.4.

■ All text fields must end somewhere. If you start a string by using a quote or an apostrophe, you must end the string with the same character. (Script 11.3). Otherwise, you'll get an error message similar to that in Figure 11.5.

Script 11.1 A script with no errors.

```
<HTML>
<HEAD>
<TITLE>Find the bug</TITLE>
<SCRIPT LANGUAGE=JAVASCRIPT>
 <!-- Hide script from older browsers
 var adImages = new Array("banner1.gif",
 →"banner2.gif","banner3.gif")
 var thisAd = 0
 var imgCt = 3

 function rotate() {
   thisAd++
   if (thisAd == imgCt) {
     thisAd = 0
   }
   document.adBanner.src=adImages[thisAd]
   setTimeout("rotate()", 3 * 1000)
 }
 // End hiding script -->
</SCRIPT>
</HEAD>
<BODY BGCOLOR=WHITE onload="rotate()">
<CENTER><IMG SRC="images/banner1.gif"
 →WIDTH="400" HEIGHT="75"
 →NAME="adBanner"></CENTER>
</BODY>
</HTML>
```

COMMON ERRORS

Script 11.2 A script with one equal sign instead of two.

```
                    script

<HTML>
<HEAD>
<TITLE>Find the bug</TITLE>
<SCRIPT LANGUAGE=JAVASCRIPT>
 <!-- Hide script from older browsers
 var adImages = new Array("banner1.gif",
 → "banner2.gif","banner3.gif")
 var thisAd = 0
 var imgCt = 3

 function rotate() {
   thisAd++
   if (thisAd = imgCt) {
     thisAd = 0
   }
   document.adBanner.src=adImages[thisAd]
   setTimeout("rotate()", 3 * 1000)
 }
 // End hiding script -->
</SCRIPT>
</HEAD>
<BODY BGCOLOR=WHITE onload="rotate()">
<CENTER><IMG SRC="images/banner1.gif"
 →WIDTH="400" HEIGHT="75"
 →NAME="adBanner"></CENTER>
</BODY>
</HTML>
```

Script 11.3 A script with unmatched quotes.

```
                    script

<HTML>
<HEAD>
<TITLE>Find the bug</TITLE>
<SCRIPT LANGUAGE=JAVASCRIPT>
 <!-- Hide script from older browsers
 var adImages = new Array("banner1.gif",
 → "banner2.gif","banner3.gif)
 var thisAd = 0
 var imgCt = 3

 function rotate() {
   thisAd++
   if (thisAd == imgCt) {
     thisAd = 0
   }
   document.adBanner.src=adImages[thisAd]
   setTimeout("rotate()", 3 * 1000)
 }
 // End hiding script -->
</SCRIPT>
</HEAD>
<BODY BGCOLOR=WHITE onload="rotate()">
<CENTER><IMG SRC="images/banner1.gif"
 →WIDTH="400" HEIGHT="75"
 →NAME="adBanner"></CENTER>
</BODY>
</HTML>
```

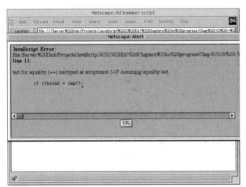

Figure 11.4 The error result of Script 11.2.

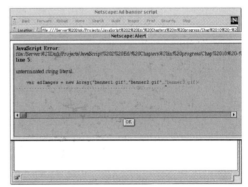

Figure 11.5 The resulting error from Script 11.3.

- When comparing two fields in an if statement, the comparison must be surrounded by parenthesis (Script 11.4). Figure 11.6 shows the error message that would display.

- Check your script carefully for typos and missing or misspelled words. Script 11.5 has a missing word, with the resulting error message shown in Figure 11.7.

- Check your script for missing punctuation. Script 11.6 has a missing "}" at the end of the function, causing the error message shown in Figure 11.8.

COMMON ERRORS

Script 11.4 This script is missing a parenthesis.

```
<HTML>
<HEAD>
<TITLE>Find the bug</TITLE>
<SCRIPT LANGUAGE=JAVASCRIPT>
 <!-- Hide script from older browsers
 var adImages = new Array("banner1.gif",
 →"banner2.gif","banner3.gif")
 var thisAd = 0
 var imgCt = 3

 function rotate() {
   thisAd++
   if (thisAd == imgCt {
     thisAd = 0
   }
   document.adBanner.src=adImages[thisAd]
   setTimeout("rotate()", 3 * 1000)
 }
 // End hiding script -->
</SCRIPT>
</HEAD>
<BODY BGCOLOR=WHITE onload="rotate()">
<CENTER><IMG SRC="images/banner1.gif"
 →WIDTH="400" HEIGHT="75"
 →NAME="adBanner"></CENTER>
</BODY>
</HTML>
```

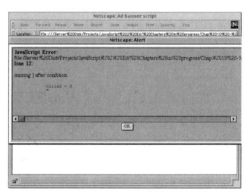

Figure 11.6 The error produced by Script 11.4.

Script 11.5 A word was left out of this script.

```
<HTML>
<HEAD>
<TITLE>Find the bug</TITLE>
<SCRIPT LANGUAGE=JAVASCRIPT>
 <!-- Hide script from older browsers
 var adImages = new Array("banner1.gif",
 →"banner2.gif","banner3.gif")
 var thisAd = 0
 var = 3

 function rotate() {
   thisAd++
   if (thisAd == imgCt) {
     thisAd = 0
   }
   document.adBanner.src=adImages[thisAd]
   setTimeout("rotate()", 3 * 1000)
 }
 // End hiding script -->
</SCRIPT>
</HEAD>
<BODY BGCOLOR=WHITE onload="rotate()">
<CENTER><IMG SRC="images/banner1.gif"
 →WIDTH="400" HEIGHT="75"
 →NAME="adBanner"></CENTER>
</BODY>
</HTML>
```

Script 11.6 Missing that last curly brace in this script.

```
<HTML>
<HEAD>
<TITLE>Find the bug</TITLE>
<SCRIPT LANGUAGE=JAVASCRIPT>
 <!-- Hide script from older browsers
 var adImages = new Array("banner1.gif",
 →"banner2.gif","banner3.gif")
 var thisAd = 0
 var imgCt = 3

 function rotate() {
   thisAd++
   if (thisAd == imgCt) {
     thisAd = 0
   }
   document.adBanner.src=adImages[thisAd]
   setTimeout("rotate()", 3 * 1000)

 // End hiding script -->
</SCRIPT>
</HEAD>
<BODY BGCOLOR=WHITE onload="rotate()">
<CENTER><IMG SRC="images/banner1.gif"
 →WIDTH="400" HEIGHT="75"
 →NAME="adBanner"></CENTER>
</BODY>
</HTML>
```

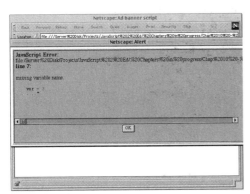

Figure 11.7 The error message caused by Script 11.5.

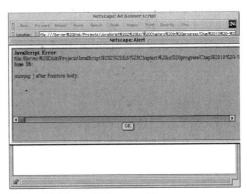

Figure 11.8 Script 11.6 causes this error message.

✔ Tips

- JavaScript is case-sensitive. This means that if you name a function callMe(), and then later reference it as callme(), you'll get an error when the function can't be found.

- Objects must exist before they can be referenced. If your header script refers to a part of the page that hasn't loaded yet, you will receive an error. For example, if you try to set a text field in a form to have a default value, but the form has not yet loaded on the page, an error will result.

- There are a number of words, such as name, that are called Reserved Words. These are words that have a special meaning to JavaScript, and so cannot be used as variable names. The full list of reserved words is in Appendix B.

- Get in the habit of indenting your scripts in a consistent way. It will make tracking down errors considerably easier.

- Curly braces ({}) are not required around single lines. However, if you always use them, you're much less likely to run into trouble when you quickly add a statement into an if block.

- It's very common to see the error message show up, realize what the problem is, switch back to your script editor, make the change, and then try to re-run the script. What happens in this case is that the script then tries to run itself in the error message window, which cannot be closed or moved to the back. Always dismiss error message windows before trying to re-run a script.

Script 11.7 Putting an alert call within a script lets you keep track of values to help track down errors.

```
                    script
<HTML>
<HEAD>
<TITLE>Find the bug</TITLE>
<SCRIPT LANGUAGE=JAVASCRIPT>
 <!-- Hide script from older browsers
 var adImages = new Array("banner1.gif",
 →"banner2.gif","banner3.gif")
 var thisAd = 0
 var imgCt = 3

 function rotate() {
   alert("The current value of thisAd is:
   →"+thisAd)
   thisAd++
   if (thisAd == imgCt) {
     thisAd = 0
   }
   document.adBanner.src=adImages[thisAd]
   setTimeout("rotate()", 3 * 1000)
 }
 // End hiding script -->
</SCRIPT>
</HEAD>
<BODY BGCOLOR=WHITE onload="rotate()">
<CENTER><IMG SRC="images/banner1.gif" WIDTH="400"
 →HEIGHT="75" NAME="adBanner"></CENTER>
</BODY>
</HTML>
```

Figure 11.9 The variable thisAd doesn't have the value we expected.

Following variables while a script is running

A script may not have an error that matches any of the messages in the previous section, but it still might not run correctly. This is often due to a logic error, where the syntax may be fine but the script itself has a problem, as in Script 11.7. Modifying the script so that the variables can be viewed while the script is running helps track down logic errors.

To view variables during script execution:

1. alert("The current value of thisAd is: " → +thisAd)

The simplest method is just to add an alert call within the problem area. This will pop up a window showing the value of whatever alert was passed. This also halts execution of the script until you dismiss the window.

✔ Tips

■ It's common to have a script that has an error, but you can't locate it. A good way to narrow down the problem is to add a call to alert before and after the problem area, then progressively move the calls closer together.

■ Instead of an alert call, you can set window.status with the message you want to display. This displays the requested values in the browser's status bar.

Viewing values in another window

Another debugging approach is to open a separate window and write all the debugging information there. This approach, shown in Script 11.8, lets you view variables without the script writing over previous values.

To write debugging info to a separate window:

1. debugWin = window.open
  → ("","debugWin","height=200,width=200,
  → resize=yes")

This opens a resizable window with the name debugWin and a height and width of 200 pixels.

2. debugWin.document.write(thisAd)

This line write out the value of the passed variable; in this case, the value of thisAd.

3. debugWin.document.close()

This line forces the result of the previous write in Step 2 to the Debug Window, as shown in Figure 11.10. JavaScript will only show the new information being written to the window when it can no longer store it internally, or when you request that it do so by sending a close(). Note that this does not close the Debug Window; it closes the document, not the window itself.

Script 11.8 You can write out values to the Debug Window while the script is running.

```
<HTML>
<HEAD>
<TITLE>Find the bug</TITLE>
<SCRIPT LANGUAGE=JAVASCRIPT>
 <!-- Hide script from older browsers
 var adImages = new Array("banner1.gif",
 →"banner2.gif","banner3.gif")
 var thisAd = 0
 var imgCt = 3
 debugWin = window.open("","debugWin",
 →"height=200,width=200,resize=yes")

 function rotate() {
   debugWin.document.write(thisAd)
   debugWin.document.close()
   thisAd++
   if (thisAd != imgCt) {
     thisAd = 0
   }
   document.adBanner.src=adImages[thisAd]
   setTimeout("rotate()", 3 * 1000)
 }
 // End hiding script -->
</SCRIPT>
</HEAD>
<BODY BGCOLOR=WHITE onload="rotate()">
<CENTER><IMG SRC="images/banner1.gif" WIDTH="400"
 →HEIGHT="75" NAME="adBanner"></CENTER>
</BODY>
</HTML>
```

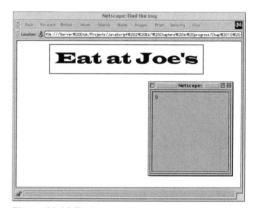

Figure 11.10 Tracking the execution of a script by writing values to a separate window is a handy debugging method.

VIEWING VALUES IN ANOTHER WINDOW

Script 11.9 This script creates a custom error window.

```
<HTML>
<HEAD>
<TITLE>Find the bug</TITLE>
<SCRIPT LANGUAGE=JAVASCRIPT>
 <!-- Hide script from older browsers
 var adImages = new Array("banner1.gif",
 →"banner2.gif","banner3.gif")
 var thisAd = 0
 var imgCt = 3
 onError = errWindow

 function errWindow(errMsg,location,lineNum) {
   debugWin = window.open("","debugWin",
   →"height=200,width=200,resize=yes")
   debugWin.document.write("<H1>There was an
   →error at line " + lineNum)
   debugWin.document.write("<br>The error was: "
   →+ errMsg)
   debugWin.document.close()
   return true
 }

 function rotate() {
   thisAd++
   if (thisAd == imgCt) {
     thisAd = 0
   }
   document.adBanner.src=adImages[thisAd]
   setTimeout("rotat()", 3 * 1000)
 }
 // End hiding script -->
</SCRIPT>
</HEAD>
<BODY BGCOLOR=WHITE onload="rotate()">
<CENTER><IMG SRC="images/banner1.gif" WIDTH="400"
 →HEIGHT="75" NAME="adBanner"></CENTER>
</BODY>
</HTML>
```

Figure 11.11 This shows the custom error message in action.

Writing error messages to another window

If you don't like your browser's error messages, you can write your own. This method, as shown in Script 11.9, lets you display values of variables as the script is aborting.

To create your own error messages:

1. onError = errWindow

The event handler onError controls what the browser does when an error is encountered. In this statement, you're telling the browser to call the function errWindow() whenever an error occurs.

2. function errWindow
→ (errMsg,location,lineNum) {

This line starts the declaration of errWindow. The browser automatically passes the error message (errMsg), the URL (location), and the approximate line number where the error occurred (lineNum). These three parameters are all required and must be in this order.

3. debugWin = window.open
→ ("","debugWin","height=200,width=200,
→ resize=yes")

This opens up a resizable Debug window, with a width and height of 200 pixels. If a window is already open with this name, JavaScript just returns a reference to it.

4. debugWin.document.write("<H1>There was
→ an error at line " + lineNum)
debugWin.document.write("
The error
→ was: " + errMsg)

These lines print the error information to the Debug Window, as shown in Figure 11.11. You can, if you choose, add any messages or variables here that you want to see just before the script ends.

(Continued)

5. debugWin.document.close()

This line ensures that everything you just wrote out is actually visible in the window.

6. return true

}

The errWindow function needs to return either true or false. True tells the browser that the error has been handled acceptably and that it does not need to also put up the standard error message. Returning false, or not returning any value at all, will cause the standard error message window to appear, along with the custom window.

✔ Tip

- If you use onError = null no message will display on the screen, no matter what errors you receive.

WHERE TO LEARN MORE

Once you've worked through this book, you should be well on your way to spicing up your Web sites with JavaScript. But there's lots more to learn about the JavaScript language, and you'll probably have questions as you write your own code.

The best place to get those questions answered is online, as you might expect. There are many resources on the Web and elsewhere on the Internet that can help you out and deepen your understanding of JavaScript.

In this chapter, we'll point you to several of the most helpful JavaScript-oriented Web sites, some Usenet newsgroups where you can interact with other scripters, and even mention a few other books that the authors found helpful.

Finding Help on the Web

The mother lode of JavaScript help is found at Netscape's Web site, but there's a lot of good information at sites from Microsoft and independent JavaScript pages. Here are some of the best JavaScript Web sites.

Netscape Sites:

Since Netscape developed JavaScript, it's no surprise that Netscape's Web site has lots of great information about the language and further development.

Netscape JavaScript Authoring Guide

http://home.netscape.com/eng/mozilla/Gold/handbook/javascript/index.html

As you can see in Figure 12.1, this site is designed for the relatively inexperienced JavaScript user. It gives you a rundown on the basics of the language, definitions and explanations of the concepts used in JavaScript, and it has a Reference section that gives you the correct syntax for each of the language's operators and features. One nice thing about this Reference section is that it includes examples for each part of the language, so that you can see how a particular part works. Overall, the JavaScript Authoring Guide is written at a moderately-geeky level, but you should be able to puzzle it out once you've digested this book. For you harder-core programming types, this site will be a piece of cake.

Figure 12.1 Netscape's JavaScript Authoring Guide is a good place for you to start furthering your knowledge of JavaScript.

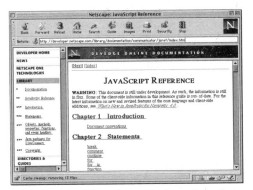

Figure 12.2 Track down the correct form of a JavaScript statement at Netscape's JavaScript Reference site.

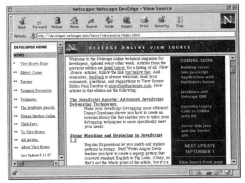

Figure 12.3 Netscape's View Source online magazine is a prime source of tips to make your JavaScript better.

Netscape JavaScript Reference

http://developer.netscape.com/library/
documentation/communicator/jsref/index.htm

This site is similar to, but not quite the same as, the Authoring Guide site. This site focuses more on the new additions to JavaScript made in Netscape 4.0 and later, and is more of a straight reference site. You'll also find information here about the work that Netscape is doing (along with many other companies) to make JavaScript a sanctioned, open standard through an international standards organization called ECMA (http://www.ecma.ch). Figure 12.2 gives you a look at the JavaScript Reference site.

✔ Tip

- Another, similar site is Netscape's JavaScript Guide site. It covers much of the same information as the sites listed above, but there's also some good information for novices. Point your browser to http://home.netscape.com/eng/mozilla/3.0/handbook/javascript/index.html

Netscape's View Source Magazine

http://developer.netscape.com/news/
viewsource/index.html

This online magazine, shown in Figure 12.3, is updated every other week, and has the latest in tips, tricks, and feature articles for developers of any Netscape products, not just JavaScript, but there's always a healthy slug of JavaScript information available.

FINDING HELP ON THE WEB

Netscape JavaScript Debugger

http://developer.netscape.com/software/
jsdebug.html

This page is considerably more advanced than the previous sites, but it gives you a valuable tool: a Java-based JavaScript debugger. Figure 12.4 shows you the page where you can get the debugger, and you can see the debugger in action in Figure 12.5. You'll need to be using Netscape Communicator 4.0 or Navigator 4.0 or later to use the debugger. You should also know that because of Netscape's Java implementation on the Macintosh, the debugger is quite slow, even on a very fast Mac. Windows 95 speed is a bit better.

Debugging tools in general aren't too useful for the short scripts that we've used through most of this book; often you'll find that it is faster and easier to debug your script with your own brainpower. For more information on debugging your JavaScript, refer to Chapter 11.

✔ Tip

■ JavaScript is far from perfect, and it has bugs of its own (they're not all in your code!). Stay abreast of JavaScript's bugs by checking Netscape's JavaScript Known Bugs List, at
http://developer.netscape.com/library/javascript/faqs/buglist/js-known-bugs.html

DevEdge Online

http://developer.netscape.com

On a more general note, Figure 12.6 shows Netscape's main page for its developer site. It's a good idea to look into this page periodically, because new tools and announcements often show up here before they get to other Netscape sites.

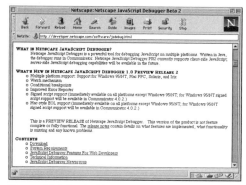

Figure 12.4 On the Netscape site, you can download a Java-based JavaScript debugger.

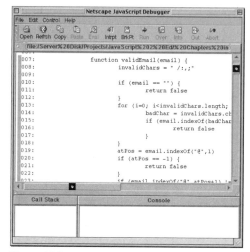

Figure 12.5 The JavaScript debugger in action.

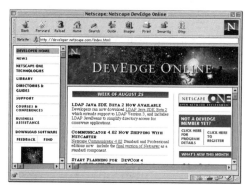

Figure 12.6 Netscape's DevEdge Online keeps you on the bleeding edge of JavaScript development.

FINDING HELP ON THE WEB

Figure 12.7 Developer.Com's JavaScript site keeps you up to date with the latest JavaScript news, and has links to some of the best JavaScript sample code and examples anywhere.

Figure 12.8 Live Software's JavaScript Resource Center has many examples that are free for the taking.

Other great JavaScript sites

When you get away from the Netscape sites, you'll find an amazing number of places where you can pick up script examples, find tutorials, and ask questions of JavaScript experts. Here are some of the best sites as of the time we wrote this, but as usual on the Web, these sites could change or even go away by the time you read this.

Developer.Com's JavaScript Site

http://javascript.developer.com/

We can't say enough great things about this site. It is updated constantly, and features some of the best JavaScript work being done by busy programmers worldwide. It has capsule descriptions and links to some very cool scripts, and they've been thoughtfully categorized for you, so you can find what you want, when you want it. Figure 12.7 gives you a look at the main screen. Notice that there's a navigation bar that gives you access to Developer.Com's sites for other Internet technologies, including Java, ActiveX, and emerging technologies such as VRML (Virtual Reality Markup Language) and the so-called push formats for automatic software distribution.

The site has a news section to keep you apprised of developments in the field, and there is an appealing "Ask the Experts" section that lets you get answers to your real stumpers.

Live Software

http://www.livesoftware.com/jrc/index.html

Live Software's JavaScript Resource Center is another terrific place to find free JavaScript samples; chances are if you have a problem with your site, you can find something here that will bring you a long way towards the solution. It also has a nice, no-nonsense design, as shown in Figure 12.8.

JavaScript World

http://www.mydesktop.com/internet/javascript/

Like the previous two sites, JavaScript World (Figure 12.9) tries to provide the most exhaustive array of resources for JavaScript. Amazingly, it comes close. The hot tickets here are the site's many tutorials and links to unusual JavaScript resources, such as IRC (Internet Relay Chat) channels that discuss scripting.

Figure 12.9 JavaScript World brings scripts from around the planet to your desktop.

Doc JavaScript

http://webreference.com/js/

The doctor is in, and he knows just what ails those sick HTML pages. Diagnosis: Too boring to live! Prescription: A healthy dose of JavaScript, and there's plenty in stock here. Prognosis: After treatment, excellent. Patient is fresher, more active, and less inclined to error. Make your appointment with the doctor, as seen in Figure 12.10. Say ahhhhhhhhh....

Figure 12.10 Heal those sickly Web pages with a trip to Doc JavaScript!

Microsoft's JScript Web Page

http://www.microsoft.com/jscript/

Microsoft's competing version of JavaScript, called JScript, has its own site (Figure 12.11), where you can learn the similarities (and differences) from Netscape JavaScript. You'll also find information here about the ECMA script standard with which JavaScript and JScript will both be compatible.

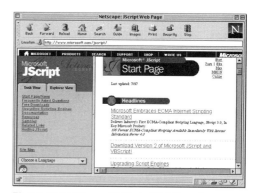

Figure 12.11 Microsoft's JScript Web Page gives you the lowdown on this JavaScript variant.

FINDING HELP ON THE WEB

Figure 12.12 The comp.lang.javascript newsgroup is a lively place to ask and answer JavaScript questions.

Usenet newsgroups

You can think of Usenet as a worldwide bulletin board system, where people from everywhere can post messages and join discussions about subjects that interest them. Each subject is called a *newsgroup*. At last count, there were more than 25,000 newsgroups, covering virtually every subject you can imagine. Naturally, we're interested here in the few newsgroups that are devoted to JavaScript.

The main Usenet newsgroup for JavaScript is news:comp.lang.javascript, where there are many discussions about scripting, people asking questions about problems that have them stymied, and general talk among JavaScript developers. It's a good place to get answers and pick up tips, as shown in Figure 12.12. Within the newsgroup, there are different discussion topics, or *threads*. You'll often find that threads begun by other people will apply to your own questions.

✔ Tip

- Usenet can be a wild place, and old-timers can be merciless to new people ("newbies") who ask what (to the old-timers) seem to be foolish questions. It's best to hang around and just read other people's messages before you post your first message in a newsgroup. You may save yourself a lot of grief and avoid many nasty messages (called flames). Never forget that your messages can be potentially read by millions of people worldwide. If one is available, read the FAQ (Frequently Asked Questions, pronounced "fack") file for the newsgroup. Chances are, you'll find that some of your questions will be answered in the FAQ, plus there's always other interesting information there. You can find the latest FAQ files for most newsgroups on the news.answers newsgroup.

USENET NEWSGROUPS

Books

Though the authors would naturally like to think that the book you've got in your hands is all you'll ever need to become a JavaScript expert, they recognize that you might just want a bit more information after you've eagerly devoured this book. There are approximately a zillion JavaScript books on the market; here are some of the books that we think are the best.

JavaScript, The Definitive Guide, Second Edition

Written by David Flanagan and published by O'Reilly & Associates, this is an exhaustive reference to the JavaScript language. Not for the faint of heart, this is the book the experts turn to look up those weird operators and nail down that odd syntax. We don't know why there is a rhinoceros on the cover of this book, however.

JavaScript Bible, Second Edition

Another clear, well-written book from Danny Goodman, this IDG Books entry explains JavaScript in detail, but in a friendlier fashion than the O'Reilly book.

Designing with JavaScript: Creating Dynamic Web Pages

Written by Nick Heinle, this is the second O'Reilly book to make our hit parade. We like this one because it deals extensively with making smart Web pages, ones that change dynamically depending on user actions.

Laura Lemay's Web Workshop: JavaScript 1.1

This book was written by Michael Moncur as part of the popular Web Workshop series from Sams.net. It's a fine book with plenty of examples.

REAL WORLD JAVASCRIPT

What is The Workbook?

The Workbook is a publishing company based in Hollywood, CA. For almost 20 years they've been publishing thick, glossy books showing the best in photography and illustration. In 1997 they launched their web site, The Workbook Online, at http://www.workbook.com/.

The site is geared to fulfill the needs of its customers: art directors and stock photography buyers. Because most visitors do not have a technical background, the site cannot depend on the users necessarily having the latest and greatest browsers. JavaScript is used to give The Workbook surfers the simplest possible site with an amazing amount of power under the hood.

Examples and exercises are fine when you're learning a new skill like JavaScript, but there's no substitute for seeing how JavaScript gets used by working programmers in the real world. This chapter takes the skills you learned in previous chapters and shows you how they are used in an actual web site.

Starting Out

When creating a JavaScript-intensive site, it's appropriate to start by checking to see if the user's browser can handle JavaScript. In Script 13.1, you'll tell the user if their browser isn't capable of handling the site, as in Figure 13.1. If the browser supports JavaScript, users see the page in Figure 13.2.

To redirect a browser based on whether it can handle JavaScript:

1. `<SCRIPT LANGUAGE=JAVASCRIPT>`

   You only want this script to be acted upon if the user has JavaScript.

2. `<!-- Hide script from old browsers`

   If visitors are using an older browser that doesn't understand JavaScript, this will make it believe that the rest of the script is a comment.

3. `// If we're JavaScript enabled, load the real`
   `→ start page`

   You're about to do something tricky, so add a comment (see Chapter 2) for future reference. In this case, browsers that can handle JavaScript are sent somewhere else.

4. `document.write('<FRAMESET COLS="100%,*"`
   `→ FRAMEBORDER=NO BORDER=0><FRAME`
   `→ SRC="index2.html" SCROLLING=AUTO>`
   `→ </FRAMESET>')`

   If you've made it to here, you know that the user's browser can handle enough JavaScript to manage the site without errors. So, create a frameset on the fly and load in the real start page (Script 13.2). This makes the browser ignore anything in the `<BODY>` area of this page.

5. `// end hiding script from old browsers -->`
   `</SCRIPT>`

   Finish off the script by ending the comment and closing the script tag.

Figure 13.1 It's not a pretty site without a JavaScript-compatible browser.

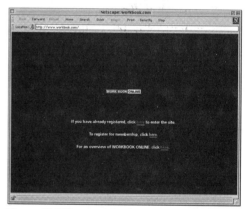

Figure 13.2 Users with JavaScript-compatible browsers see this and don't even know that they've just passed a test.

✔ Tip

■ A browser can be current enough to support JavaScript, but still have JavaScript turned off. Figure 13.1 warns people that this may be the case.

Script 13.1 This script checks to see if the user has a newer browser and has JavaScript enabled, and then throws them to the real start page. Otherwise, it lets them know they just don't have what it takes.

```
script
<HTML>
<HEAD>
 <TITLE>workbook.com</TITLE>
 <SCRIPT LANGUAGE=JAVASCRIPT>
 <!-- Hide script from old browsers
   // If we're JavaScript enabled, load the real start page
 document.write('<FRAMESET COLS="100%,*" FRAMEBORDER=NO BORDER=0><FRAME SRC="index2.html" SCROLLING=AUTO>
→'</FRAMESET>')
 // end hiding script from old browsers -->
 </SCRIPT>
</HEAD>

<BODY BGCOLOR="#000000" TEXT="#FFFFFF" LINK="#FFFFFF" VLINK="#FFFFFF">
<TABLE BORDER=0 WIDTH="100%" HEIGHT="100%" CELLPADDING=0 CELLSPACING=0>
<TR>
 <TD ALIGN=RIGHT>
  <IMG SRC="http://www.workbook.com/img/bad_site1.gif" WIDTH=301 HEIGHT=343><BR>
 </TD>
 <TD WIDTH=300>
  <BR><IMG SRC="http://www.workbook.com/img/
→bad_site2.gif" WIDTH=253 HEIGHT=81><BR>
  <IMG SRC="http://www.workbook.com/img/
→workbook_logo.gif" WIDTH=111 HEIGHT=14
→VSPACE=20>
  <FONT FACE="b frutiger bold,helvetica,arial"
→SIZE=-1><P>This site makes use of progressive
→JPEG, JavaScript, client-side imagemaps, and
→enhanced tables and frames.</P>
  <P>You either have JavaScript disabled, or you
→aren't using the latest version of Netscape
→Navigator, so please upgrade now... we wouldn't
→want you to miss out!</P>
  <P>If you would like to continue without Netscape
→3.0, click <A HREF="/home2.html">here</A>.</P>
<A HREF="http://home.netscape.com/comprod/mirror/
→index.html" TARGET="ext"><IMG SRC="http://
→www.workbook.com/netnow3.gif" VSPACE=10
→BORDER=0 HEIGHT=31 WIDTH=88></A><BR>
  Click <A HREF="ftp://ftp.netscape.com/pub/
→Navigator/3.01/shipping/english/mac">here</A>
→to download Netscape 3.01 for Macintosh.<BR>
  Click <A HREF="ftp://ftp.netscape.com/pub/
→Navigator/3.01/shipping/english/windows">
→here</A> to download Netscape 3.01 for Windows.
→</FONT>
 </TD>
</TR>
</TABLE>
</BODY>
</HTML>
```

Script 13.2 The script of the actual start page.

```
<HTML>
<HEAD>
 <TITLE>workbook.com</TITLE>
</HEAD>
<BODY BGCOLOR="#000000">
 <P ALIGN=CENTER>
 <TABLE WIDTH=100% HEIGHT=100% BORDER=0
CELLSPACING=0 CELLPADDING=0>
   <TR><TD WIDTH=100%><CENTER>
   <TABLE WIDTH=678 HEIGHT=374 BORDER=0
CELLSPACING=0 CELLPADDING=0>
    <TR><TD WIDTH=100%><P ALIGN=CENTER>
    <A HREF="home2.html" TARGET="_TOP"><IMG
    SRC="http://www.workbook.com/img/splash_logo2
    .gif" WIDTH=129 HEIGHT=79 BORDER=0 VSPACE=14
    ALIGN=BOTTOM></A></P>
    <P><BR></P><P ALIGN=CENTER>
    <A HREF="home2.html" TARGET="_TOP">
    →<IMG SRC="http://www.workbook.com/img/
    →intro1.gif" WIDTH=328 HEIGHT=17 BORDER=0
    →VSPACE=7></A><BR>
    <A HREF="newuser.html" TARGET="_TOP">
    →<IMG SRC="http://www.workbook.com/img/
    →intro2.gif" WIDTH=216 HEIGHT=15 BORDER=0
    →VSPACE=15></A><BR>
    <A HREF="site_guide.html" TARGET="_TOP">
    →<IMG SRC="http://www.workbook.com/img/
    →intro3.gif" WIDTH=292 HEIGHT=16 BORDER=0
    →VSPACE=7></A>
    </TD></TR>
   </TABLE>
   </TD></TR>
 </TABLE>
</BODY>
</HTML>
```

Giving users feedback with JavaScript

One of the main uses of JavaScript is to give a user feedback about an action they can take. The menu screen in Script 13.3 uses image rollovers and sounds to make users aware of their options.

To give a user feedback:

1. bName = navigator.appName
bVer = parseInt(navigator.appVersion)
loadSounds = false

Initialize the variables, so that **bName** is the name of the browser, **bVer** is the browser version, and **loadSounds** is false.

2. if (bName == "Netscape" && bVer >= 4 &&
→ navigator.appVersion.indexOf("68k") == –1
→ && navigator.javaEnabled()) {
    loadSounds = true
}

If the browser is Netscape 4 or later, the user is not running on a pre-PowerPC Mac, and Java is enabled, then re-initialize **loadSounds** to be true.

3. function playSound(SName) {
    if (loadSounds &&
    → document.embeds[SName] != null &&
    → document.embeds[SName].IsReady()) {
        document.embeds[SName].play(false)
    }
}

When **playSound** is passed the name of a sound, it checks to see if the browser has loaded sounds for this page, and if the sound is ready to play. If all the tests are passed, the sound is played.

(Continued)

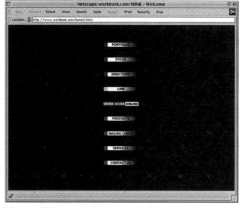

Figure 13.3 A nice clean menu, with no clutter.

Script 13.3 A menu that gives users feedback about their choices.

```
                              script
<HTML>
<HEAD>
 <TITLE>workbook.com: HOME - Welcome
 </TITLE>
<SCRIPT LANGUAGE=JAVASCRIPT>
 <!-- Hide script from old browsers
 bName = navigator.appName
 bVer = parseInt(navigator.appVersion)
 loadSounds = false

 // Set flag to use later on whether or not we want to bother loading in the sounds
 if (bName== "Netscape" && bVer >= 4 && navigator.appVersion.indexOf("68k") == -1 &&
 ⇥navigator.javaEnabled()) {
   loadSounds = true
 }

 // This function detects the ability to play LiveAudio and then decides
 // whether or not to play a specified embed's sound file.
 function playSound(SName) {
   if (loadSounds && document.embeds[SName] != null && document.embeds[SName].IsReady()) {
     document.embeds[SName].play(false)
   }
 }

 // Turn off Netscape's error checking.
 onerror = null

 // Pre-load the rollover graphics
 if (document.images) {
   contact_us_glow = new Image
   contact_us_glow.src = "http://www.workbook.com/img/home2/contact_us_glow.gif"
   contact_us_off = new Image
   contact_us_off.src = "http://www.workbook.com/img/home2/contact_us.gif"
   contact_us_text = new Image
   contact_us_text.src = "http://www.workbook.com/img/home2/contact_us_text.gif"

   directory_glow = new Image
   directory_glow.src = "http://www.workbook.com/img/home2/directory_glow.gif"
   directory_off = new Image
   directory_off.src = "http://www.workbook.com/img/home2/directory.gif"
   directory_text = new Image
   directory_text.src = "http://www.workbook.com/img/home2/directory_text.gif"

   line_glow = new Image
   line_glow.src = "http://www.workbook.com/img/home2/line_glow.gif"
   line_off = new Image
   line_off.src = "http://www.workbook.com/img/home2/line.gif"
   line_text = new Image
   line_text.src = "http://www.workbook.com/img/home2/line_text.gif"

   mailing_labels_glow = new Image
   mailing_labels_glow.src = "http://www.workbook.com/img/home2/mailing_labels_glow.gif"
   mailing_labels_off = new Image
   mailing_labels_off.src = "http://www.workbook.com/img/home2/mailing_labels.gif"
   mailing_labels_text = new Image
   mailing_labels_text.src = "http://www.workbook.com/img/home2/mailing_labels_text.gif"

   portfolio_glow = new Image
   portfolio_glow.src = "http://www.workbook.com/img/home2/portfolio_glow.gif"
   portfolio_off = new Image
   portfolio_off.src = "http://www.workbook.com/img/home2/portfolio.gif"
   portfolio_text = new Image
   portfolio_text.src = "http://www.workbook.com/img/home2/portfolio_text.gif"
```

(Script continues on page 160.)

Script 13.3 (continued)

```
                                  script

   products_glow = new Image
   products_glow.src = "http://www.workbook.com/img/home2/products_glow.gif"
   products_off = new Image
   products_off.src = "http://www.workbook.com/img/home2/products.gif"
   products_text = new Image
   products_text.src = "http://www.workbook.com/img/home2/products_text.gif"

   services_glow = new Image
   services_glow.src = "http://www.workbook.com/img/home2/services_glow.gif"
   services_off = new Image
   services_off.src = "http://www.workbook.com/img/home2/services.gif"
   services_text = new Image
   services_text.src = "http://www.workbook.com/img/home2/services_text.gif"

   stock_glow = new Image
   stock_glow.src = "http://www.workbook.com/img/home2/stock_glow.gif"
   stock_off = new Image
   stock_off.src = "http://www.workbook.com/img/home2/stock.gif"
   stock_text = new Image
   stock_text.src = "http://www.workbook.com/img/home2/stock_text.gif"

   newText = new Image
   newText.src = "http://www.workbook.com/img/home2/blank.gif"
}
else {
   document.port = ""
   document.stock = ""
   document.directory = ""
   document.line = ""
   document.products = ""
   document.mailing_labels = ""
   document.services = ""
   document.contact_us = ""
   document.text = ""
   newText = ""

   contact_us_glow = ""
   contact_us_off = ""
   contact_us_text = ""

   directory_glow = ""
   directory_off = ""
   directory_text = ""

   line_glow = ""
   line_off = ""
   line_text = ""

   mailing_labels_glow = ""
   mailing_labels_off = ""
   mailing_labels_text = ""

   portfolio_glow = ""
   portfolio_off = ""
   portfolio_text = ""

   products_glow = ""
   products_off = ""
   products_text = ""

   services_glow = ""
   services_off = ""
   services_text = ""
```

(Script continues on page 161.)

GIVING USERS FEEDBACK WITH JAVASCRIPT

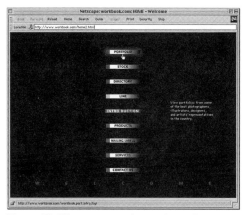

Figure 13.4 If users want to know what each option leads to, they simply put the cursor over a menu item and a description appears.

4. `<A HREF="/workbook.port.intro.fcgi"`
   → `OnMouseOver="playSound('bark'),`
   → `document.port.src=portfolio_glow.src,`
   → `document.text.src=portfolio_text.src"`
   `OnMouseOut="document.port.src=`
   → `portfolio_off.src, document.text.src=`
   → `newText.src">`
   `<IMG SRC= "http://www.workbook.com/`
   → `img/home2/portfolio.gif" HEIGHT=44`
   → `WIDTH=138 ALIGN=BOTTOM BORDER=0`
   → `NAME= port></A>`

When the user puts the cursor over the "portfolio" button (as in Figure 13.4), three things happen: (1) playSound is called, with a parameter of "bark," (2) the portfolio image itself is overwritten with a glowing version of itself, and (3) explanatory text is shown in the text area. When the cursor moves off the portfolio button, the image is returned to its non-glowing state, and the text area returns to black (see Figure 13.3 on page 158).

(Continued)

Script 13.3 *(continued)*

```
    stock_glow = ""
    stock_off = ""
    stock_text = ""
 }
 // end hiding script from old browsers -->
</SCRIPT>
</HEAD>

<BODY BGCOLOR=BLACK TOPMARGIN=0 LEFTMARGIN=0>

<TABLE WIDTH="100%" HEIGHT="100%" BORDER=0 CELLPADDING=0 CELLSPACING=0>
<TR>
<TD ALIGN=MIDDLE><TABLE WIDTH=678 BORDER=0 CELLSPACING=0 CELLPADDING=0 HEIGHT=374>
<TR>
<TD HEIGHT=350 WIDTH=225> </TD>
<TD WIDTH=226><P ALIGN=CENTER>

 <A HREF="/workbook.port.intro.fcgi" OnMouseOver="playSound('bark'), document.port.src=portfolio_glow.src,
 ↪document.text.src=portfolio_text.src"
 OnMouseOut="document.port.src=portfolio_off.src, document.text.src=newText.src">
 <IMG SRC="http://www.workbook.com/img/home2/portfolio.gif" HEIGHT=44 WIDTH=138 ALIGN=BOTTOM BORDER=0
 ↪NAME=port></A><BR>

 <A HREF="/intro_stock.html" OnMouseOver="playSound('bark'), document.stock.src=stock_glow.src,
 ↪document.text.src=stock_text.src"
 OnMouseOut="document.stock.src=stock_off.src, document.text.src=newText.src">
 <IMG SRC="http://www.workbook.com/img/home2/stock.gif" HEIGHT=44 WIDTH=138 ALIGN=BOTTOM BORDER=0
 ↪NAME=stock></A><BR>
```

(Script continues on page 163.)

GIVING USERS FEEDBACK WITH JAVASCRIPT

5. if loadSounds {
    document.write("<EMBED SRC=
    → '/sounds/bark.au' NAME=bark
    → HIDDEN=TRUE LOOP=FALSE
    → AUTOSTART=FALSE MASTERSOUND>")
    document.write("<EMBED SRC=
    → '/sounds/pop.au' NAME=pop
    → HIDDEN=TRUE LOOP=FALSE
    → AUTOSTART=FALSE MASTERSOUND>")
    document.write("<EMBED SRC=
    → '/sounds/urp.au' NAME=urp
    → HIDDEN=TRUE LOOP=FALSE
    → AUTOSTART=FALSE MASTERSOUND>")
}

When a user has a slow Internet connection, every byte sent from your server to their machine counts against you. In this case, you know that sounds are only going to be played under certain circumstances—so why load them if they're not going to be played? This body script checks the previously initialized variable loadSounds to decide whether to write the three <EMBED> tags out at all.

✔ Tips

- JavaScript 1.1 browsers can handle sounds, so why limit this script to JavaScript 1.2 browsers? In this case, it's because the events that cause the sounds to be played are within a table, and while JavaScript 1.1 browsers understand sounds and tables, they don't understand sounds within tables.

- LiveAudio does not support pre-PowerPC Macs, so you need to skip them by checking the appVersion of Navigator.

- More than one thing can be done when processing OnMouseOver and OnMouseOut (and other similar) events. Just put a comma between the commands as shown in step 4.

GIVING USERS FEEDBACK WITH JAVASCRIPT

Script 13.3 *(continued)*

```
<A HREF="/intro_directory.html" ONMOUSEOVER="playSound('bark'),
→document.directory.src=directory_glow.src, document.text.src=directory_text.src"
ONMOUSEOUT="document.directory.src=directory_off.src, document.text.src=newText.src">
<IMG SRC="http://www.workbook.com/img/home2/directory.gif" HEIGHT=44 WIDTH=138 ALIGN=BOTTOM BORDER=0
→NAME=directory></A><BR>

<A HREF="/line/index.html" ONMOUSEOVER="playSound('urp'), document.line.src=line_glow.src,
→document.text.src=line_text.src"
ONMOUSEOUT="document.line.src=line_off.src, document.text.src=newText.src">
<IMG SRC="http://www.workbook.com/img/home2/line.gif" HEIGHT=44 WIDTH=138 ALIGN=BOTTOM BORDER=0
→NAME=line></A><BR>

<A HREF="/site_guide.html"><IMG SRC="http://www.workbook.com/img/home2/animated_logo.gif" VSPACE=16
→HEIGHT=12 WIDTH=109 BORDER=0></A><BR>

<A HREF="/products/index.html" ONMOUSEOVER="playSound('pop'), document.products.src=products_glow.src,
→document.text.src=products_text.src"
ONMOUSEOUT="document.products.src=products_off.src, document.text.src=newText.src">
<IMG SRC="http://www.workbook.com/img/home2/products.gif" HEIGHT=44 WIDTH=138 ALIGN=BOTTOM BORDER=0
→NAME=products></A><BR>

<A HREF="/mailing_labels/index.html" ONMOUSEOVER="playSound('pop'),
→document.mailing_labels.src=mailing_labels_glow.src, document.text.src=mailing_labels_text.src"
ONMOUSEOUT="document.mailing_labels.src=mailing_labels_off.src, document.text.src=newText.src">
<IMG SRC="http://www.workbook.com/img/home2/mailing_labels.gif" HEIGHT=44 WIDTH=138 ALIGN=BOTTOM BORDER=0
→NAME=mailing_labels></A><BR>

<A HREF="/services/index.html" ONMOUSEOVER="playSound('pop'), document.services.src=services_glow.src,
→document.text.src=services_text.src"
ONMOUSEOUT="document.services.src=services_off.src, document.text.src=newText.src">
<IMG SRC="http://www.workbook.com/img/home2/services.gif" HEIGHT=44 WIDTH=138 ALIGN=BOTTOM BORDER=0
→NAME=services></A><BR>

<A HREF="/services/contact.html" ONMOUSEOVER="playSound('pop'),
→document.contact_us.src=contact_us_glow.src, document.text.src=contact_us_text.src"
ONMOUSEOUT="document.contact_us.src=contact_us_off.src, document.text.src=newText.src">
<IMG SRC="http://www.workbook.com/img/home2/contact_us.gif" HEIGHT=44 WIDTH=138 ALIGN=BOTTOM BORDER=0
→NAME=contact_us></A><BR>

</TD>
<TD WIDTH=226><P ALIGN=CENTER>
<IMG SRC="http://www.workbook.com/img/home2/blank.gif" WIDTH=159 HEIGHT=59 ALIGN=BOTTOM
→NAME=TEXT></TD></TR><TR><TD COLSPAN=3><P ALIGN=CENTER>
<IMG SRC="http://www.workbook.com/img/home2/welcome_home.gif" WIDTH=545 HEIGHT=11 ALIGN=BOTTOM
→VSPACE=12></TD>

<SCRIPT LANGUAGE="JAVASCRIPT1.2">
  <!-- Hide script from old browsers

  if loadSounds {
    document.write("<EMBED SRC='/sounds/bark.au' NAME=bark HIDDEN=TRUE LOOP=FALSE
    AUTOSTART=FALSE MASTERSOUND>")
    document.write("<EMBED SRC='/sounds/pop.au' NAME=pop HIDDEN=TRUE LOOP=FALSE AUTOSTART=FALSE
    →MASTERSOUND>")
    document.write("<EMBED SRC='/sounds/urp.au' NAME=urp HIDDEN=TRUE LOOP=FALSE AUTOSTART=FALSE
    →MASTERSOUND>")
  }
  // end hiding script from old browsers -->
</SCRIPT>
</TR></TABLE>
<IMG SRC="http://www.workbook.com/img/spacer.gif" WIDTH=678 HEIGHT=1><BR>
</TD></TR></TABLE>
</BODY>
</HTML>
```

Sharing a .js file

If two pages share identical JavaScripts, it makes sense to put the common script elements in a ".js" file and have both pages reference that file. This way, a change to the single file updates both HTML pages.

To share a .js file:

1. <SCRIPT LANGUAGE=JAVASCRIPT
   → SRC="/portButtons.js">
   </SCRIPT>

   The <SCRIPT> tag appears as normal, but with the addition of an additional attribute: SRC. This is set to the path of the .js file that contains the JavaScript for the page. Both Script 13.4 (Figure 13.5) and Script 13.5 (Figure 13.6) reference the JavaScript in Script 13.6. This script, in portButtons.js, controls the twinkling buttons on both pages.

✔ Tips

- The server must be configured to serve the .js file correctly. If your pages have trouble with this command, check with your provider to see if this is the problem.

- This method is sometimes used to try to hide JavaScripts from users. It doesn't work if the user is technically savvy enough to check their browser cache files—everything that the browser has seen is stored there.

- This is the one time that you don't have to include the lines to comment out JavaScript for older browsers. The older browsers don't know enough to ever look within the .js file.

- You can put more than one header script in a page. It's perfectly acceptable to have one page refer to multiple .js files and still contain the script elements unique to that page.

Figure 13.5 This page allows the user to change the portfolio category they wish to view. The buttons twinkle; a random one changes 5 times per second.

Figure 13.6 The introductory page to the portfolio section contains the same buttons that are in the previous figure, with identical functionality.

Script 13.4 Because the JavaScript is kept in a common file, this script is much shorter than if it were not shared.

```
                                      script
<HTML>
<HEAD>
 <TITLE>
   workbook.com: PORTFOLIO - Change Category
 </TITLE>
 <SCRIPT LANGUAGE=JAVASCRIPT SRC="/portButtons.js">
 </SCRIPT>
</HEAD>
<BODY LINK=BLACK VLINK=BLACK BGCOLOR=WHITE ONLOAD="rotate()">
<MAP NAME="port_intro_buttons">
 <AREA SHAPE="rect" COORDS="0,0,40,20" HREF="/site_guide/portfolio_map.html">
 <AREA SHAPE="rect" COORDS="50,0,93,21" HREF="/map.html">
 <AREA SHAPE="rect" COORDS="101,0,149,21" HREF="/home.html">
</MAP>
<TABLE WIDTH="100%" HEIGHT="100%"><TR><TD>
<CENTER><TABLE WIDTH=678 BORDER=0>
 <TR><TD ALIGN=CENTER COLSPAN=5><IMG SRC="http://www.workbook.com/img/cat_change_instruction.gif"
→HEIGHT=19 WIDTH=325><P><BR></P></TD>
 </TR>
 <TR><TD ALIGN=CENTER WIDTH=20%>
   <A HREF="/priv/portfolio/photo.html"><IMG SRC="http://www.workbook.com/img/photo/button_00.jpg"
   →NAME=photo BORDER=0></A>
 </TD>
 <TD ALIGN=CENTER WIDTH=20%>
   <A HREF="/priv/portfolio/ill.html"><IMG SRC="http://www.workbook.com/img/ill/button_00.jpg" NAME=ill
   →BORDER=0></A>
 </TD>
 <TD ALIGN=CENTER WIDTH=20%>
   <A HREF="/priv/portfolio/design.html"><IMG SRC="http://www.workbook.com/img/design/button_00.jpg"
   →NAME=design BORDER=0></A>
 </TD>
 <TD ALIGN=CENTER WIDTH=20%>
   <A HREF="/priv/portfolio/digital.html"><IMG SRC="http://www.workbook.com/img/digital/button_00.jpg"
   →NAME=dig BORDER=0></A>
 </TD>
 <TD ALIGN=CENTER WIDTH=20%>
   <A HREF="/priv/portfolio/rep.html"><IMG SRC="http://www.workbook.com/img/reps/button_00.jpg" NAME=rep
   →BORDER=0></A>
 </TD>
 </TR>
 <TR>
  <TD ALIGN=CENTER><B><FONT FACE="geneva,helvetica,arial" SIZE=1>PHOTOGRAPHY</FONT></B></TD>
  <TD ALIGN=CENTER><B><FONT FACE="geneva,helvetica,arial" SIZE=1>ILLUSTRATION</FONT></B></TD>
  <TD ALIGN=CENTER><B><FONT FACE="geneva,helvetica,arial" SIZE=1>DESIGN</FONT></B></TD>
  <TD ALIGN=CENTER><B><FONT FACE="geneva,helvetica,arial" SIZE=1>DIGITAL</FONT></B></TD>
  <TD ALIGN=CENTER><B><FONT FACE="geneva,helvetica,arial" SIZE=1>ARTISTS' REPS</FONT></B></TD>
 </TR></TABLE></CENTER>

<P><BR></P>
<P ALIGN=CENTER>

<IMG SRC="http://www.workbook.com/img/intro_buttons.gif" ALIGN=MIDDLE USEMAP="#port_intro_buttons"
→BORDER=0></TD></TR></TABLE>
</BODY>
</HTML>
```

SHARING A .JS FILE

Script 13.5 This script shares the common JavaScript with Script 13.4.

```
<HTML>
 <HEAD>
 <TITLE>workbook.com: PORTFOLIO
 </TITLE>
 <SCRIPT LANGUAGE=JAVASCRIPT SRC="/portButtons.js">
 </SCRIPT>
</HEAD>
<BODY BGCOLOR=WHITE ONLOAD="rotate()">
 <MAP NAME="intro_buttons">
   <AREA SHAPE=RECT COORDS='0,0,44,14' HREF="/site_guide/portfolio_map.html">
   <AREA SHAPE=RECT COORDS='50,0,94,14' HREF="/map.html">
   <AREA SHAPE=RECT COORDS='100,0,144,14' HREF="/home.html">
 </MAP>
 <TABLE WIDTH=100% HEIGHT=100% BORDER=0 CELLSPACING=0 CELLPADDING=0>
 <TR><TD>
 <CENTER><TABLE WIDTH=678 BORDER=0 CELLSPACING=0 CELLPADDING=0>
 <TR VALIGN=TOP><TD COLSPAN=2 BGCOLOR=BLACK>
   <IMG SRC="http://www.workbook.com/img/port_intro_logo.gif" HSPACE=7 VSPACE=25 WIDTH=172 HEIGHT=35
 ALIGN=ABSMIDDLE>
 </TD><TD BGCOLOR=BLACK ALIGN=RIGHT VALIGN=MIDDLE>
   <IMG SRC="http://www.workbook.com/img/intro_buttons.gif" HSPACE=7 WIDTH=144 HEIGHT=14 ALIGN=ABSMIDDLE
 USEMAP="#intro_buttons" BORDER=0>
 </TD></TR>
 <TR><TD COLSPAN=3 ALIGN=CENTER>
   <IMG SRC="http://www.workbook.com/img/port_copy.gif" WIDTH=633 HEIGHT=13 VSPACE=12>
 </TD></TR>
 <TR VALIGN=TOP><TD>
   <FONT SIZE=-1 FACE="geneva,helvetica,arial">
   Alexander/Pollard<BR>
   Appleton, Doug<BR>
   The Art Source<BR>
   Aspinall, Neal<BR>
   Barton, Paul<BR>
   Bender, Brenda<BR>
   Berenholtz, Richard<BR>
   Biondo Productions<BR>
   Bobbe, Leland<BR>
   Borowski, Diane<BR>
   Braun, Kathy Represents<BR>
   Brown, Laura<BR>
   Buckley, Dana<BR>
   Burke, Robert<BR>
   </FONT>
 </TD>
 <TD>
   <FONT SIZE=-1 FACE="geneva,helvetica,arial">
   Burke/Triolo<BR>
   Burnett, Yolanda Represents<BR>
   Bush, Charles (Chas) W.<BR>
   Bybee Studios<BR>
   Carr, E. J.<BR>
   Casemore, Rick<BR>
   Caton, Chip<BR>
   Chromagen<BR>
   Cleveland, Thomas<BR>
   Cohn, Carol Reps<BR>
   Collins, Daryll<BR>
   Comport, Allan WC Studio<BR>
```

(Script continues on page 167.)

```
                                              script

    Comport, Sally Wern<BR>
    Connor, Tom<BR>
    </FONT>
  </TD>
  <TD>
    <FONT SIZE=-1 FACE="geneva,helvetica,arial">
    Cornell, Kathleen & Company<BR>
    Covington, N. K.<BR>
    Covington, Neverne<BR>
    Coxwell, Chris<BR>
    Crocker, Will<BR>
    Crowley, Eliot<BR>
    Darling, Scott<BR>
    Davis, Dennas<BR>
    DiVitale Photography<BR>
    DLM Artist Representatives<BR>
    Empress Bowling League, The<BR>
    Envoy, Inc.<BR>
    Epstein, Rhoni Photographers' Reps<BR>
    Evenson Design<BR>
    <P ALIGN=RIGHT><A HREF="workbook.port.intro.fcgi?4">next</A> >>
    </FONT>
  </TD></TR>
  </TABLE><P><BR></P>
  <TABLE WIDTH=678>
  <TR><TD ALIGN=CENTER WIDTH=20%>
    <A HREF="/priv/portfolio/photo.html"><IMG SRC="http://www.workbook.com/img/photo/button_01.jpg"
 →NAME=photo BORDER=0></A>
  </TD>
  <TD ALIGN=CENTER WIDTH=20%>
    <A HREF="/priv/portfolio/ill.html"><IMG SRC="http://www.workbook.com/img/ill/button_01.jpg" NAME=ill
 →BORDER=0></A>
  </TD>
  <TD ALIGN=CENTER WIDTH=20%>
    <A HREF="/priv/portfolio/design.html"><IMG SRC="http://www.workbook.com/img/design/button_01.jpg"
 →NAME=design BORDER=0></A>
  </TD>
  <TD ALIGN=CENTER WIDTH=20%>
    <A HREF="/priv/portfolio/digital.html"><IMG SRC="http://www.workbook.com/img/digital/button_01.jpg"
 →NAME=dig BORDER=0></A>
  </TD>
  <TD ALIGN=CENTER WIDTH=20%>
    <A HREF="/priv/portfolio/rep.html"><IMG SRC="http://www.workbook.com/img/reps/button_01.jpg" NAME=rep
 →BORDER=0></A>
  </TD></TR>
  <TR>
    <TD ALIGN=CENTER><B><FONT FACE="geneva,helvetica,arial" SIZE=1>PHOTOGRAPHY</FONT></B></TD>
    <TD ALIGN=CENTER><B><FONT FACE="geneva,helvetica,arial" SIZE=1>ILLUSTRATION</FONT></B></TD>
    <TD ALIGN=CENTER><B><FONT FACE="geneva,helvetica,arial" SIZE=1>DESIGN</FONT></B></TD>
    <TD ALIGN=CENTER><B><FONT FACE="geneva,helvetica,arial" SIZE=1>DIGITAL</FONT></B></TD>
    <TD ALIGN=CENTER><B><FONT FACE="geneva,helvetica,arial" SIZE=1>ARTISTS' REPS</FONT></B></TD>
  </TR></TABLE></CENTER>
</TD></TR></TABLE>
</BODY>
</HTML>
```

Script 13.6 The script shared by Script 13.4 and Script 13.5.

```
portButtons.js
// This file contains the JavaScript for animating portfolio category buttons.
// It is used by both cat_change.html & workbook.port.intro.fcgi

var firstTime = 1

photoButton = new Array
illButton = new Array
digButton = new Array
designButton = new Array
repButton = new Array
imgArray = new Array

for (i=0; i<2; i++) {
 photoButton[i] = new Image
 illButton[i] = new Image
 digButton[i] = new Image
 designButton[i] = new Image
 repButton[i] = new Image
}

   // Pre-load the animated graphics
if (document.images) {
 photoButton[0].src = "http://www.workbook.com/img/photo/button_00.jpg"
 photoButton[1].src = "http://www.workbook.com/img/photo/button_01.jpg"

 illButton[0].src = "http://www.workbook.com/img/ill/button_00.jpg"
 illButton[1].src = "http://www.workbook.com/img/ill/button_01.jpg"

 digButton[0].src = "http://www.workbook.com/img/digital/button_00.jpg"
 digButton[1].src = "http://www.workbook.com/img/digital/button_01.jpg"

 designButton[0].src = "http://www.workbook.com/img/design/button_00.jpg"
 designButton[1].src = "http://www.workbook.com/img/design/button_01.jpg"

 repButton[0].src = "http://www.workbook.com/img/reps/button_00.jpg"
 repButton[1].src = "http://www.workbook.com/img/reps/button_01.jpg"

 imgArray = new Array(photoButton[0], photoButton[1], illButton[0], illButton[1], designButton[0],
designButton[1], digButton[0], digButton[1], repButton[0], repButton[1])
}
else {
 document.photo = ""
 document.ill = ""
 document.dig = ""
 document.design = ""
 document.rep = ""
}

function rotate() {
 if (firstTime == 1) {
   buttonArray = new Array(document.photo, document.ill, document.design, document.dig, document.rep)
   lastButton = -1
   firstTime = 0
 }

 randomImg = Math.floor(Math.random() * 10)
 randomButton = Math.floor(randomImg / 2)
 if (lastButton != randomButton) {
   buttonArray[randomButton].src = imgArray[randomImg].src
   lastButton = randomButton
 }
 setTimeout('rotate()',200)
}
```

APPENDIX A:
JavaScript
Genealogy
and Reference

JavaScript has been transformed over the past few years, since its introduction as part of Netscape Navigator 2.0. This appendix briefly discusses the different versions of JavaScript, and which browsers include which version.

You'll also find a JavaScript object flowchart as well as a table listing all of the JavaScript software objects up to JavaScript version 1.2, along with their properties, methods, and event handlers.

JavaScript versions

The first version of JavaScript, originally called LiveScript, was first released in Netscape Navigator 2.0. Netscape intended LiveScript to be a way to extend the capabilities of browsers, and to allow Web designers to add some interactivity to their sites. The JavaScript version in Navigator 2.0 is JavaScript 1.0.

Along with Navigator 3.0 came JavaScript 1.1, which added support for arrays, Java applets, and plug-ins, among many other changes.

With the release of Navigator 4.0 (also known as Netscape Communicator), JavaScript 1.2 was born, with more enhancements and refinements. (See Table A.2 for details of the new features of JavaScript 1.2.)

All three of these versions (1.0, 1.1, and 1.2) are the *client-side* versions of JavaScript; that is, they are embedded in Web browsers, and only work within browsers. But JavaScript is actually a quite powerful programming language, and it could be used in situations appropriate for most other programming languages. Since there isn't exactly a screaming need for another general-purpose programming language in the world, there are few other applications for JavaScript outside of browsers. One notable exception is LiveWire, the programming language built into the Web server software that Netscape sells. LiveWire (sometimes called *server-side JavaScript*) is based on JavaScript 1.0, with additional extensions that let it work well in the server environment. For example, LiveWire has connections to high-end databases; a compiler to speed code execution; and features that ease server management. LiveWire can substitute for other scripting languages such as Perl that provide CGI scripts on Web servers. There are versions of LiveWire for Windows 95, Windows NT, and Unix. Netscape doesn't offer their server software for the Mac OS.

JScript

As is so often the case, Microsoft implemented JavaScript in its own fashion, which is not always compatible with the Netscape version. Called JScript version 1, the Microsoft version of JavaScript is more-or-less compatible with JavaScript 1.0; there are some differences. Naturally, JScript appears only in versions of Microsoft Internet Explorer (MSIE).

On Windows, there is a JScript version 2 for Windows 95/NT that works in upgraded versions of MSIE 3.02 and later. Not all versions of MSIE 3.02 have JScript 2.0. In order to tell what version of JScript you have installed, search your disk for 'jscript.dll'. Get the file's properties, and click on the Version tab. If the file version does not begin with 2, then you should download an updater from Microsoft, or upgrade to MSIE 4.0.

On the Macintosh, MSIE 3.0 has no JScript; you'll need to download version 3.01 from http://www.microsoft.com/msdownload/ieplatform/iemac.htm. This includes JScript 1.0, but not the identical version as on Windows; there are differences between the Mac and Windows version of JScript (for example, the Mac version supports the Image object for mouse rollovers, while the Windows JScript 1.0 does not).

Confused yet? You're in good company. But wait, there's more: MSIE 4.0 (for Windows 95/NT; as of this writing the Mac 4.0 implementation is unreleased) includes JScript 3.0, with a new set of features, which you can learn about at http://www.microsoft.com/sitebuilder/workshop/prog/ie4/jscript3-f.htm. Even a partial explanation of JScript 3.0 is beyond the scope of this appendix, but it is roughly equivalent to JavaScript 1.2.

ECMAScript

In 1996, Web developers began to complain that Netscape was going in one direction with JavaScript, and Microsoft in a somewhat-compatible but different direction with JScript. Nobody likes to have to code pages to handle different dialects of JavaScript, or have their code work in one browser, but not another. Developers wanted a standard. So Netscape went to an international standards body called ECMA and submitted the JavaScript language specification to them, and Microsoft threw in their own comments and suggestions. ECMA did whatever it is that standards bodies do and in June of 1997 produced a standard called ECMA-262 (also known as ECMAScript, a term that just dances off the tongue). This standard closely resembles JavaScript 1.1, but (sigh) is not exactly the same. If you're interested in reading the official ECMAScript specification, you can download it from http://www.ecma.ch/stand/ecma-262.htm.

Microsoft claims that Internet Explorer 4.0 is ECMAScript-compliant, plus some extra, proprietary features that are specific to MSIE 4.0. So as long as you write ECMAScript-compatible code, it should run just fine under MSIE 4.0 and probably Netscape Navigator 3.0 and later. But you should always test your code with different browsers, platforms, and versions just to be sure.

At this writing, no Netscape browser claims to be 100% ECMAScript compliant. If by all this explanation you leap to the conclusion that the ECMAScript "standard" is honored more in the breach than to the letter, you won't be far off the mark.

Browsers and JavaScript

The following table shows you which versions of which browsers support a given version of JavaScript. This table is just a rough guide, because as mentioned in the JScript section above, Mac and Windows implementations of JScript have been different.

Table A.1

Browsers and their JavaScript versions	
BROWSER	JAVASCRIPT VERSION
Netscape Navigator 2.0x	1.0
Netscape Navigator 3.0x	1.1
Netscape Navigator 4.0x*	1.2
Microsoft Internet Explorer 3.0x	1.0
Microsoft Internet Explorer 4.0x	1.2

*All versions of Netscape Communicator include Navigator 4.0.

Object flowchart

JavaScript objects are connected together in a particular order, which you can think of in terms of an organization chart. The primary object in JavaScript is the current window, and all other software objects flow from that window, as seen in Figure A.1. This order of objects is often called *the JavaScript object hierarchy*, but that name is just a tad too self-important for this book.

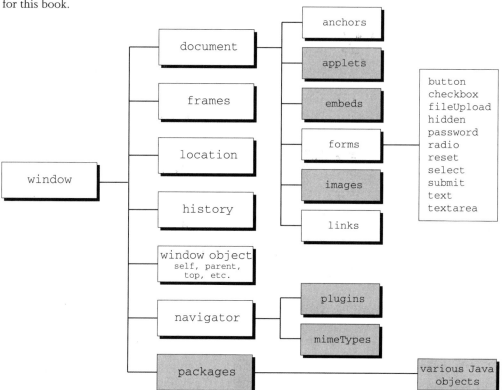

Figure A.1 The object flowchart acts like a map of the way you can string JavaScript objects together. Objects marked in gray are new to Navigator 3.0 (i.e., JavaScript 1.1).

OBJECT FLOWCHART

The big object table

No JavaScript book is complete without the whopping big table of all of the JavaScript objects, along with their associated properties, methods, and event handlers (check Chapter 1 for definitions of these terms). The table included here covers most of the JavaScript objects in the language up through JavaScript 1.2. We've omitted a few very obscure objects, and some older objects from earlier versions that have been superseded by new or extended objects in version 1.2. In Table A.2, the entries marked in gray are only available in JavaScript 1.2, and will only work reliably (if at all) in Navigator 4.0 or MSIE 4.0 or later.

Table A.2

JavaScript Object Table

Object	Properties	Methods	Event handlers
Anchor	none	none	none
anchors array	length	none	none
Applet	none	applet's methods	none
applets array	length	none	none
Area	hash	none	onClick
	host		onMouseOut
	hostname		onMouseOver
	href		
	pathname		
	port		
	protocol		
	search		
	target		
Array	length	concat	none
		join	
		reverse	
		slice	
		sort	
Button	form	blur	onBlur
	name	click	onClick
	type	focus	onFocus
	value		
Checkbox	checked	blur	onBlur
	defaultChecked	click	onClick
	form	focus	onFocus

JavaScript Object Table *(continued)*

OBJECT	PROPERTIES	METHODS	EVENT HANDLERS
Checkbox *(continued)*	name		
	type		
	value		
Date	none	getDate	none
		getDay	
		getHours	
		getMinutes	
		getMonth	
		getSeconds	
		getTime	
		getTimezoneOffset	
		getYear	
		parse	
		setDate	
		setHours	
		setMinutes	
		setMonth	
		setSeconds	
		setTime	
		setYear	
		toGMTString	
		toLocaleString	
		toString	
		UTC	
		valueOf	
document	alinkColor	close	none
	Anchor	captureEvents	
	anchors	getSelection	
	Applet	open	
	applets	releaseEvents	
	Area	routeEvents	
	bgColor	write	
	cookie	writeln	
	domain		
	embeds		
	fgColor		
	Form		
	forms		
	Image		
	images		
	lastModified		
	linkColor		
	Link		

JavaScript Object Table *(continued)*

OBJECT	PROPERTIES	METHODS	EVENT HANDLERS
document *(continued)*	links referrer title URL vlinkColor		
FileUpload	form name type value	blur focus	onBlur onChange onFocus
Form	action Button Checkbox elements encoding FileUpload Hidden length method name Password Radio Reset Select Submit target Text Textarea	reset submit	onReset onSubmit
forms array	length	none	none
Frame	frames name length parent self window	blur clearInterval clearTimeout focus print setInterval setTimeout	onBlur onFocus
frames array	length	none	none
Hidden	name type value	none	none
History	current length next previous	back forward go	none

	JavaScript Object Table (continued)		

OBJECT	PROPERTIES	METHODS	EVENT HANDLERS
history array	length	none	none
Image	border	none	onAbort
	complete		onError
	height		onLoad
	hspace		
	lowsrc		
	name		
	src		
	vspace		
	width		
images array	length	none	none
	hash	none	onClick
	host		onMouseOut
	hostname		onMouseOver
	href		
	pathname		
	port		
	protocol		
	search		
	target		
links array	length	none	none
location	hash	reload	none
	host	replace	
	hostname		
	href		
	pathname		
	port		
	protocol		
	search		
Math	E	abs	none
	LN2	acos	
	LN10	asin	
	LOG2E	atan	
	LOG10E	atan2	
	PI	ceil	
	SQRT1_2	cos	
	SQRT2	exp	
		floor	
		log	
		max	
		min	
		pow	
		random	

JAVASCRIPT OBJECT TABLE

JavaScript Object Table *(continued)*

Object	Properties	Methods	Event handlers
Math *(continued)*		round	
		sin	
		sqrt	
		tan	
MimeType	description	none	none
	enabledPlugin		
	type		
	suffixes		
mimeTypes array	length	none	none
navigator	appCodeName	javaEnabled	none
	appName	preference	
	appVersion	taintEnabled	
	language		
	mimeTypes		
	platform		
	plugins		
	userAgent		
Number	none	none	none
options array	length	none	none
options array elements	defaultSelected	none	none
	index		
	length		
	selected		
	selectedIndex		
	text		
	value		
Password	defaultValue	blur	onBlur
	form	focus	onFocus
	name	select	
	type		
	value		
Plugin	description	none	none
	filename		
	length		
	name		
plugins array	length	refresh	none
Radio	checked	blur	onBlur
	defaultChecked	click	onClick
	form	focus	onFocus
	length		
	name		
	type		
	value		

JAVASCRIPT OBJECT TABLE

JavaScript Object Table *(continued)*			
OBJECT	**PROPERTIES**	**METHODS**	**EVENT HANDLERS**
Reset	form	blur	onBlur
	name	click	onClick
	type	focus	onFocus
	value		
screen	availHeight	none	none
	availWidth		
	colorDepth		
	height		
	pixelDepth		
	width		
Select	form	blur	onBlur
	length	focus	onChange
	name		onFocus
	options		
	selectedIndex		
	text		
	type		
String	length	anchor	none
		big	
		blink	
		bold	
		charAt	
		charCodeAt	
		concat	
		fixed	
		fontcolor	
		fontsize	
		fromCharCode	
		indexOf	
		italics	
		lastIndexOf	
		link	
		match	
		replace	
		search	
		slice	
		small	
		split	
		strike	
		sub	
		substr	
		substring	
		sup	

JavaScript Object Table *(continued)*

OBJECT	PROPERTIES	METHODS	EVENT HANDLERS
String *(continued)*		toLowerCase	
		toUpperCase	
Submit	form	blur	onBlur
	name	click	onClick
	type	focus	onFocus
	value		
Text	defaultValue	blur	onBlur
	form	focus	onChange
	name	select	onFocus
	type		onSelect
	value		
Textarea	defaultValue	blur	onBlur
	form	focus	onChange
	name	select	onFocus
	type		onSelect
	value		
window	closed	alert	onBlur
	defaultStatus	back	onError
	document	blur	onFocus
	Frame	captureEvents	onLoad
	frames	clearInterval	onUnload
	history	clearTimeOut	
	innerHeight	close	
	innerWidth	confirm	
	length	disableExternalCapture	
	location	enableExternalCapture	
	locationbar	find	
	menubar	focus	
	name	forward	
	opener	home	
	outerHeight	moveBy	
	outerWidth	moveTo	
	pageXOffset	open	
	pageYOffset	releaseEvents	
	parent	resizeBy	
	personalbar	resizeTo	
	scrollbars	routeEvents	
	self	print	
	status	prompt	
	statusbar	scrollBy	
	toolbar	scrollTo	
	top	stop	
	window	setInterval	
		setTimeOut	

Appendix B: JavaScript Reserved Words

Reserved words are words that have special meaning to JavaScript. Therefore, they cannot be used as variable or function names.

You'll recognize many of the reserved words from previous chapters, but others will be unfamiliar. Some of the latter group are future reserved words; i.e., it's expected that they'll be commands in future versions of JavaScript. They're being set aside now so that you won't have to revise your code when new revisions are released.

JavaScript reserved words:

These words are part of the JavaScript language.

break	if	true
continue	in	var
else	new	void
false	null	while
for	return	with
function	this	

Java keywords reserved by JavaScript:

These words are used by the Java language, and are reserved in JavaScript to avoid possible confusion.

abstract	final	private
boolean	finally	protected
byte	float	public
case	goto	short
catch	implements	static
char	import	super
class	instanceOf	switch
const	int	synchronized
default	interface	throw
do	long	throws
double	native	transient
extends	package	try

Additional words reserved by ECMAScript:

These words are part of the ECMAScript language specification (see Appendix A for more on ECMAScript).

delete	typeOf

Additional reserved words proposed to be used by ECMAScript:

These words have been reserved because they may be used in future versions of ECMAScript.

debugger	enum	export

JAVASCRIPT RESERVED WORDS

Other identifiers to avoid:

These words aren't officially reserved, but as they are part of the JavaScript language, you shouldn't use them as function or variable names. If you do, abandon all hope; the results will be unpredictable.

alert	History	Packages
Anchor	Image	parent
Area	isNaN	parseFloat
Array	java	parseInt
assign	JavaArray	Password
blur	JavaClass	Plugin
Boolean	JavaObject	prompt
Button	JavaPackage	prototype
Checkbox	length	Radio
clearTimeout	Link	ref
close	location	Reset
closed	Location	scroll
confirm	Math	Select
Date	MimeType	self
defaultStatus	name	setTimeout
document	navigate	status
Document	navigator	String
Element	Navigator	Submit
escape	netscape	sun
eval	Number	taint
FileUpload	Object	Text
focus	onBlur	Textarea
Form	onError	top
Frame	onFocus	toString
frames	onLoad	unescape
Function	onUnload	untaint
getClass	open	valueOf
Hidden	opener	window
history	Option	Window

Netscape is case-sensitive, which means that it differentiates between Document and document. In Netscape, the former could in theory be used as a variable, but the latter could not. Internet Explorer is not case-sensitive, which means that it does not understand any difference between Document and document. This is why both capitalized and lower case versions of some variables are listed above.

INDEX

INDEX

INDEX

INDEX

Z